Kinky Friedman's guide to
Texas etiquette

| DATE DUE | | | |
|---|---|---|---|
| | | | |
| | | | |
| | | | |
| | | | |
| | | | |
| | | | |
| | | | |
| | | | |
| | | | |
| | | | |
| | | | |
| | | | |
| | | | |

# KINKY FRIEDMAN'S

## GUIDE
### TO

# TEXAS ETIQUETTE

# ALSO BY KINKY FRIEDMAN

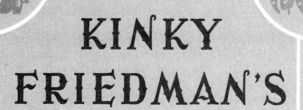

# KINKY FRIEDMAN'S

## GUIDE TO

# TEXAS ETIQUETTE

### OR

*How to Get to Heaven or Hell
Without Going Through
Dallas–Fort Worth*

Cliff Street Books

*An Imprint of* HarperCollins*Publishers*

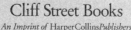

FIRST EDITION

*Designed by Mary Austin Speaker*

Library of Congress Cataloging-in-Publication Data
    Friedman, Kinky.
        Kinky Friedman's guide to Texas etiquette, or How to get
    to heaven or hell without going through Dallas–Fort Worth /
    Kinky Friedman.—1st ed.
            p. cm.
        ISBN 0-06-620988-9
        1. Texas—Social life and customs—Humor. 2. Texas—
        Description and travel—Humor. 3. Texas—History—
        Humor. I. Title: Guide to Texas etiquette. II. Title: How to
        get to heaven or hell without going through Dallas–Fort
        Worth.
    F386.6 .F75 2001
    976.4—dc21
                                                              2001028711

01 02 03 04 05 /QM/ 10  9  8  7  6  5  4  3  2  1

*13.31 B&T 09/01*

# CONTENTS

# ACKNOWLEDGMENTS

The author would like to thank the following Americans for their help with this book: Diane Reverand, Janet Dery, and all the fine folks at HarperCollins; and my agents, David Vigliano and Dean Williamson.

The author would also like to say "Thank you kindly" to the following Texans for their valuable assistance: Madge Reid, Sage Ferrero, Max Swafford, Marcie Friedman, and Billy Joe Shaver.

The author would also like to thank Don Imus for taking the photo of the author, and Wyatt Imus for letting the author borrow his cowboy bib.

# A BIG HOWDY FROM KINKY THE FRIENDLY COWBOY

Howdy, neighbor! Texas is the Friendship State and y'all are our neighbors whether you like it or not. Now I know we may seem a little loud sometimes and perhaps even a bit crude, but you've got to admit we're friendly. You might even think we look funny in our cowboy hats and our brontosaurus-foreskin boots, but we can't help the way we look. Our heroes have always been cowboys. And everybody knows what state gave the world the cowboy. Sorry, New Jersey is the wrong answer.

I know there's a lot of Yankees (and other foreigners) out there who are more curious than usual about Texas now that George W. is up there in the White House. They want to know if it's really true that Texans have a lot of wide open spaces between their ears. Being the oldest living Jew in Texas who doesn't own any real estate, I figured I'd write this book to answer any questions about what Texans believe, how Texans behave, and what exactly is Texas Etiquette. Keep in mind, of course, what I always like to say: "It's no disgrace to come from Texas; it's just a disgrace to have to go back there." (Just kiddin', folks!)

It is my hope, nevertheless, that *Kinky Friedman's Guide to Texas Etiquette* will help teach the rest of the world how to act right, like we do in Texas. I also hope this book will become a financial pleasure for the Kinkster, but that's not really the important thing. As we say in Texas, "Money may buy you a fine dog, but only love can make it wag its tail."

# THINGS YOU WOULD *NEVER* HEAR A REAL TEXAN SAY

I think that song needs more French horn.

★

Is that tuna dolphin-safe?

★

The tires on that truck are too big.

★

There's no place in my home for obscenity!

★

I believe the proper word is "African-American."

★

I'll have the decaf latte, please.

★

William Robert, you appall me.

★

This red wine has a rather cheeky bouquet.

★

I've got two cases of Perrier for the Super Bowl.

★

Fried pig rinds are disgusting.

★

You're watching football? Change the channel—
Oprah is on!

★

Will you go ahead with a home birth if the baby
arrives in Paris?

☆

Duct tape won't fix that.

☆

Honey, I think we should sell the pickup
and buy a family sedan.

☆

Come to think of it, I'll have a Heineken.

☆

We don't keep firearms in this house.

☆

You can't feed that to the dog.

☆

I thought Graceland was tacky.

☆

No kids in the back of the pickup; it's just not safe.

☆

Wrestling is not real.

☆

# BIG HAIR FOR JESUS

Anyone who has spent any time at all in the Lone
Star State has seen, and possibly interacted with,
the creature known as the Texas Big Hair. These
women spend hours to attain the perfect altitude;

their big hair techniques are as secret as family recipes and are often handed down from mother to daughter. Many non-Texans have tried to imitate the Texas Big Hair, but few have succeeded. An entire generation of heavy metal artists coveted the sheer majesty of the Texas Big Hair, but none was able to re-create it successfully in all its glory.

Fortunately for anyone reading this, I have become privy to an old family recipe for molding the perfect big hair, hair so big you would need KY jelly to wear a hat. Even the family cat will hiss at it. Be forewarned, however. This is not for amateurs. Make sure someone you trust is nearby just in case anything goes wrong.

## INGREDIENTS

one case of hair spray, preferably Set and
Spray lacquer (Aqua Net will do in a pinch)

✦

one teasing comb, extra-large curlers
(or you can use empty Coke cans)

✦

a Styrofoam cup

✦

one bag of bobby pins (at least 100)

✦

one ponytail rubber band

★

a beehive hairnet if desired
(available at drugstores and beauty supply shops)

★

Before you do anything, wash your hair, because it's
not going to get washed again for at least two weeks
no matter which Big Hair style you choose.

### BIG HAIR STYLE 1: THE BEEHIVE.

Carefully dry your hair. Put it back into a
ponytail, tight against your head. Take the
Styrofoam cup and place it on top of your
head. Curl the ponytail around the cup and
secure it using at least eighty-five bobby
pins. Spray with the lacquer until the smoke
alarm goes off.

### BIG HAIR STYLE 2: THE B-52.

After washing your hair, rinse it with sugar
water so it will dry stiffer. Take extra-large
hair curlers (or empty Coke cans) and roll
your hair with as many as you can fit on your
head. Put enough spray on your hair so that
you can actually feel the weight.

### BIG HAIR STYLE 3: THE TEXAN

Take the teasing comb and back-comb all
your hair until it looks like an electrified

Persian cat. To tease your hair, grab a small section and hold it up by the end. Comb downward with the teasing comb in short fast strokes until it gets tangled at the bottom. Pull the teased hair up and out to achieve maximum altitude. Liberally apply the hair spray to hold the teased hair in place. If you can still see the walls, you haven't sprayed enough. Spray more. All these styles must be taken care of while you sleep. Some women use the beehive hairnet; others use feather pillows to sleep upon; while still others sleep upright in the La-Z-Boy. Your mileage may vary. Just be careful not to put anyone's eye out.

## LEGEND OF THE TEXAS BLUEBONNET

Once, long ago in the land of the Comanche, there was a great drought and famine and pestilence. The dancers danced to the sound of the drums and prayed for rain. They watched and waited for the healing rains, and danced again. No rains came.

Among the children of the tribe there was a small girl named She-Who-Is-Alone. She watched the dancers and held her warrior doll. Her doll wore beaded leggings and a headdress of brilliant blue feathers from the bird who cries "jay-jay." She loved this doll very much. Her doll was the only thing she had left from the happy days before the great famine took her parents and grandparents from her.

As She-Who-Is-Alone sat and held her doll, the Shaman, or Wise Man, came to speak to the people. He told them that the Great Spirits were unhappy. He said that the people had been selfish, taking everything from the earth and giving nothing in return. He said that the people must make a sacrifice and must make a burnt offering of their most prized possession. The Shaman said the ashes of this offering should be scattered to the home of the Four Winds—North, South, East, and West. When this sacrifice was made, the drought would cease. Life would be restored to the land.

The people talked among themselves. The warriors were sure it was not their bow that the Great Spirits wanted. The women knew it was not their special blanket. She-Who-Is-Alone looked at her doll, her most valued possession. She knew what the Great Spirits wanted and knew what she must do.

While everyone slept she took her warrior doll and one stick that burned from the tepee fire and made her way to the hill where the Shaman had spoken— "O Great Spirits," she called out, "here is my warrior doll, the only thing I have left from happy days with my family. It is my most valued possession. Please accept it."

Then she made a fire and thrust her precious doll into it. When the flames died down, she scooped up a handful of ashes and scattered them to the Four Winds—North, South, East, and West. Then, her cheeks wet with tears, she lay down and fell asleep.

The first light of morning woke her and she looked out over the hills. Stretching from all sides where the ashes had fallen, the ground was covered with flowers, beautiful blue flowers, as blue as the feathers in the hair of her beloved doll.

Every spring after that, the Great Spirits remembered the sacrifice of a very small girl and filled the hills and valleys of the land now called Texas with beautiful blue flowers. And this is so to this very day.

# REDNECK, GOOD OL' BOY, OR OILMAN: WHICH KIND OF TEXAN ARE YOU?

Answer the following questions as best you can. When you are finished with the quiz, tally up your points to see which kind of Texan you are.

1. When you hear the word "mobile," you think of:
   A. your home
   B. your cousin's gas station
   C. your cell phone

2. You drive
   A. your common-law wife crazy
   B. a Ford F-150
   C. a big ol' Cadillac

3. When you burp, you
   A. recite the entire alphabet
   B. say "pardon me, ma'am"
   C. order another chicken-fried steak

4. You have a bumper sticker that says
   A. My Mother Is an Honor Student at George
      Bush Junior High
   B. God Bless John Wayne
   C. Vote Republican, It's Less Taxing

5. In tough situations you ask yourself
   A. "What would Jesus do?"
   B. "What would J. R. Ewing do?"
   C. "What would Jett Rink do?"

6. Your Mama taught you
   A. how to blow smoke rings
   B. how to read by using the Bible
   C. how to apply for depletion loans

7. One of your children was born
    A. on a pool table
    B. while you were on a hunting trip
    C. with a silver spoon in his mouth

8. Your favorite Christmas present was
    A. a black velvet painting of Elvis
    B. a bedliner for your pickup truck
    C. a Mexican trophy wife

9. Supper last night was
    A. fried bologna sandwich on white bread with mayo
    B. barbecue you cooked yourself on your own pit
    C. a 15-ounce Black Angus steak

10. Your children
    A. have the same homeroom teacher as you
    B. are full-time ranchers
    C. are waiting for you to die so they can inherit your
       fortune

**Scoring:** If you answered mostly A's, you are a red-neck. If you answered mostly B's, you are a good ol' boy. If you answered mostly C's, you are an Oilman.

# HOMETOWN HEROES

For those curious as to where the hometown heroes came from in Texas, the following is a list of notables.

| | |
|---|---|
| 1. Janis Joplin | Port Arthur |
| 2. Steve Martin | Waco |
| 3. Tommy Lee Jones | San Saba |
| 4. Kenneth Starr | Vernon |
| 5. Joan Crawford | San Antonio |
| 6. Howard Hughes | Houston |
| 7. Holly Golightly | Tulip |
| 8. Dwight D. Eisenhower | Denison |
| 9. Don Henley | Linden |
| 10. Buddy Holly | Lubbock |
| 11. Dan Rather | Wharton |
| 12. Barry White | Galveston |
| 13. F. Murray Abraham | El Paso |
| 14. Roy Orbison | Wink |
| 15. Mary Martin | Weatherford |
| 16. Van Cliburn | Fort Worth |
| 17. Willie Nelson | Abbott |
| 18. Farah Fawcett | Houston |

"Maw, I love you because your gorgeous,
sexy, and a heck of a gate opener!"

# GUIDE TO TEXAS ETIQUETTE

I'll tell you, folks, it wasn't like this at the horsepital. They served us rabbit food and astronaut food, and if you asked for five-alarm chili or a chicken-fried steak, they'd look at you like you were crazy, which, of course, most of us were. Not only did they not have any Texas food, they didn't have any Texas music either. Maybe a band like the Shalom Retirement Village People would come by once in a while, but that was about it. So I resigned from the human race for a while, and it was then that I began seeing the rather uncanny parallels between my life and the life of Jesus.

Both of us were skinny little boogers. Both of us belonged to the Jewish persuasion. Neither of us was ever married. Neither of us ever had a home to speak of. Hell, neither of us ever held a job in our lives. We both just traveled around the countryside irritating people.

When I told all this to the people at the horsepital, it irritated them as well. They weren't as friendly as the folks back in Texas. They didn't seem as

> "To the six and a half billion people on this planet who are not Texans, the very idea of Texas Etiquette may seem like a contradiction in terms."

down-to-earth either. And when you're from a state as big as Texas, it's hard to make small talk. Still, I'd walk up to somebody and ask him: "Where'd you go to school at?" He'd look at me like I was an idiot, and he'd say something like: "Where I went to school we learned never to end a sentence with a preposition." Then I'd have to say: "OK, where'd you go to school at, asshole?" And that would usually start a fight. The problem was those folks just didn't understand Texas Etiquette.

To the six and a half billion people on this planet who are not Texans, the very idea of Texas Etiquette may seem like a contradiction in terms. These unfortunate culturally deprived souls, sometimes known as the rest of the world, go blithely through life believing implicitly in lady wrestlers, Catholic universities, and military intelligence, yet they scoff at the notion of Texas Etiquette. They'd sooner believe in fairies. And everybody knows what happens to a fairy in Texas. A big cowboy with a belt buckle about the size of a license plate comes along and stomps the shit out of him and sticks one of his wings in his cowboy hat and then strikes a kitchen match on his jeans, burns a watermelon in somebody's front yard and maybe a synagogue or two, and then lights up a Marlboro.

It should be noted, of course, that fairies are not real. It should also be noted that anyone who stomps the shit out of any creature great or small is, of course, not a real cowboy. But let's get back to Texas Etiquette.

We Texans believe if it ain't King James, it ain't Bible. We believe in holding hands and saying grace before eating big hairy steaks in chain restaurants. If the steak is the size of a sombrero, the meal is followed by the belching of the Lord's Prayer, which is almost immediately followed by projectile vomiting. Extreme cases may result in what some Texans commonly refer to as "squirtin' out of both ends."

And now we move as gracefully as possible, going with the flow from culinary matters to urinary matters. The only thing that really differentiates Texas from any other place in the world is the proclivity of its people to urinate out-of-doors and to attach a certain amount of importance to this popular pastime. Urinating outside goes much further than merely meeting the criterion of what is socially acceptable; it is the way of our people. To walk out under the Texas stars and water your lizard is considered the most sacred inalienable right of all citizens of the Lone Star State.

As a matter of spiritual trivia, though it may or may not have relevance here, it should be

> "If it ain't King James, it ain't Bible!"

"Jake I promise if you won't blow any more
smoke in my face, I ain't gonna spit any
tobaccer juice in yores!"

noted that LBJ's favorite song during the time he was
president was "Raindrops Keep Fallin' on My
Head." More to the point, if you're urinating outside
anywhere in the great State of Texas (always be careful never to take a whiz on an electric fence) it is
very much within the realm of acceptable behavior.
If a stranger comes upon you—not sexually, of
course—he'll by and large leave you alone. If you're
urinating say, on the shoulder of the highway,

passersby may be seen to nod their approval, some even honking encouragement from their vehicles.

Texas, as most people know, has lived under six flags, which can create a high degree of cultural attention deficit disorder. If there's one thing we Texans know about destiny, it is that you can't count on it forever. Maybe that's why Texans always seem to look out for one another. The following is an incident that I believe illustrates this brotherhood in action. I witnessed it many years ago as I drove by an old mission in San Antonio in my Yom Kippur Clipper. (That's a Jewish Cadillac—it stops on a dime and it picks it up.)

There was a large statue of Jesus in the courtyard of the mission, and I saw a wealthy Texas rancher-type praying to it. These are the words I heard him say: "Jesus! Please help me! My Cadillacs are all in the shop! My oil wells have run dry! The cattle got the blight! The IRS is after me!" The man appeared to have a litany of troubles. And then he hears a voice on the other side of the statue and he gets up and walks around and there's a little bitty

> "The only thing that really differentiates Texas from any other place in the world is the proclivity of its people to urinate out-of-doors and to attach a certain amount of importance to this popular pastime."

Mexican praying to the same statue of Jesus. And the Mexican is saying: "Jesus, please help me! My wife is pregnant. We already have twelve children. I've just lost my job. Now we'll lose our house. And now I learn that my wife is sick. I just don't know what to do." The wealthy Texan walks over and pulls out his billfold. He takes a hundred-dollar bill out of his billfold and he hands it across to the little Mexican. "Here you go, little buddy," he says. "Don't be botherin' Jesus with that shit."

Though Texans are always a relatively considerate bunch, things do seem to get a little wiggy when a certain type of woman meets another woman from the same substratum whom she hasn't seen since Kennedy was croaked in Dallas, which we don't really consider to be part of Texas. The announcement of Kennedy's death, by the way, was reportedly greeted with cheers by the members of the Petroleum Club in Houston, which, of course, was a mild lapse of Texas Etiquette. So, no doubt, was killing President Kennedy.

As I was saying before I heard voices in my head, there is a traditional greeting used by women in Texas who haven't seen each other in a while. In sort of a latent lesbian mating ritual the first one's face lights up insanely, and she shrieks: "Look at *yeeew!*" The other one,

> "If there's one thing we Texans know about destiny, it is that you can't count on it forever."

her countenance locked in an equally demonic rictus, responds: "Look at *yeeew!!!*" There is little doubt that this increasingly frenetic, insectine

**"Jesus! Please help me! My Cadillacs are all in the shop!"**

exchange would continue indefinitely if not for the intercession of a third party.

Fortunately, a big cowboy walks up, strikes another match on his wranglers—he has two Mexican wranglers who work for him—and proceeds to set the two women on fire, mistaking them for a black church.

Now the women are dancing around like vapid versions of Joan of Arc, sparks flying from their big hair, still screaming "Look at *yeeew!*" and the two of them would've no doubt been bugled to Jesus in tandem if not for the intercession of a third party.

Fortunately, a man nearby just happens to be urinating out of doors and saves the day and the women by taking the thing into his own hands and pissing on the fire with Hose Number One.

But Texas Etiquette has its practical applications as well, and sometimes these manifestations occur far beyond the vaunted boundaries of the Lone Star State. Texas Etiquette, indeed, may have saved me from grievous bodily harm in a personal incident which I will now relate to any reader who has not been placed into a coma by the mounting ennui already generated by the tedious nature of the subject matter itself. No doubt, however, there are still a few pathological Americans who remain in the full-crouch position waiting to discover the precise nature of this wonderful personal incident. That is why, in fact, Texas Etiquette exists, if, in truth, it does. It gives us more ridiculous bullshit to believe in. It's a bit like the time Jesus brought Lazarus back to life and asked him to describe heaven and the afterlife. "You just lie there waiting to be worm-bait," Lazarus reportedly said. "There's no heaven. There's no afterlife. There's nothing at all." Jesus hurriedly put his finger to his lips. "Shhhh," he whispered. "I know."

In the mid-1960s I graduated from the University of Texas in Austin and joined the Peace Corps, where I worked for two years in the jungles of Borneo as an agricultural extension worker. My job was to help people who'd been farming successfully for over two thousand years to improve their agricultural methods. This work required copious amounts of Texas Etiquette, especially since the job required my distributing seeds downriver to the natives and in two and a half years the Peace Corps failed to send me any seeds. Eventually, I was forced to distribute my own seed downriver. which resulted in some rather unpleasant repercussions. By this time, I was fresh out of any brand of etiquette and had decided to take a little R&R trip to Thailand with a few other Peace Corps volunteers.

This was the height of the Haight-Ashbury era and also the Vietnam era. In a little seedy bar in

**"Let Saigons be bygones."**

Chiang Mai, Thailand, these two forces inexorably came together. By forces, I mean *special* forces, as in Green Berets. A group of them, on R&R from Vietnam, apparently, had been drinking rather heavily at the bar. There were four of us Peace Corps kids, all skinny as Jesus, with long hair and native beads, and one of our party, Dylan "Clitorious" Ferrero, happened, rather unfortunately, to be sporting a flower in his hair. And in the air, the sense of impending doom was almost palpable. It was the year of our Lord 1967. The Green Berets, like ourselves, had been culturally out where the buses don't run for possibly a little too long. They thought we were real hippies. And they were in no mood to let Saigons be bygones.

The smallest member of any gang of bullies is usually the one with the most to prove, and that was true in this case. A wiry, dangerous-looking little Hawaiian guy wandered over with a glaze of hatred in his eyes that almost wilted Dylan's flower. I remember his words quite well even now because he chanted them with a soft, evil cadence: "Ain't you cool."

A bar in Chiang Mai, Thailand, could be a godless, lawless place in 1967, almost as lawless and godless as a gravel road outside Jasper, Texas, in 1999. But it was just at that moment that I thought I

> "Courtesy is owed. Respect is earned. Love is given."

heard a familiar accent— a Texas accent. The deep drawling tones were emanating from the largest man I'd ever seen in my life. He was sitting with the Green Berets watching the ongoing tension convention at the bar. With a sudden confidence that must have come from deep in the heart of Texas, I left the bar and walked over to a tableful of cranked-up Special Forces. With my beads and Angela Davis Afro, it would've been the stupidest thing I'd ever done in my life, if I hadn't been so sure that Goliath was from Texas. And if the two of us had been from California or New Jersey or Lower Baboon's Asshole, I don't think it would have worked. Texas saved me.

In a matter of moments, I had learned the guy was from Dublin, Texas, and my old college friend Lou Siegel was from Dublin and the big guy knew Lou and the next thing anybody knew was that the invisible bond of latent homosexual Texas manhood had transcended all the other human chemistry in the bar and the world.

Years later, I thanked Lou Siegel for being spiritually in the right place at the right time. I never saw Goliath the Green Beret again. Maybe he just got Starbucked into the twenty-first century like everybody else and is sipping a decaf latte somewhere and reading the *Wall Street Gerbil*.

I wish I could say that Texas Etiquette really exists. Maybe it's something like God or Santa Claus or brotherly love that no one's ever seen but just might be there after all. Years ago, my mother had a little sign on her desk at Echo Hill Ranch, a summer camp for boys and girls. It read: "Courtesy is owed. Respect is earned. Love is given."

That may be as close to Texas Etiquette as any of us will ever get.

# HOW BIG *IS* TEXAS?

The Dallas/Fort Worth airport is larger than New York City's Manhattan Island.

The State Capitol located in Austin is the nation's largest statehouse, with a dome seven feet taller than that of the National Capitol in Washington, D.C.

Forty-one counties in Texas are each larger than the state of Rhode Island.

The land area of Texas is larger than all of New England, New York, Pennsylvania, Ohio, and Illinois combined.

The San Jacinto Monument in Deer Park (just outside Houston) is among the tallest columns in the world; at 570 feet, it's about 20 feet higher than the Washington Monument in the District of Columbia.

This place shore oughta be a National Park...
ain't no trees or mountains or nothin'
clutterin' up the scenery.

## ACTUAL QUOTES FROM
## ACTUAL TEXAS POLITICIANS

1. "If English was good enough for Jesus Christ, then it's good enough for Texans."

   —MA FERGUSON, FIRST WOMAN GOVERNOR OF TEXAS

2. "Lemme give ya' a hypothetic."

   —TEXAS REPRESENTATIVE RENAL ROSSON

3. "Fellow citizens, follow me into yonder saloon."

—THE SHORTEST CAMPAIGN SPEECH IN TEXAS HISTORY

4. "And now, will y'all stand and be recognized?"

—TEXAS HOUSE SPEAKER GIB LEWIS TO A GROUP OF
HANDICAPPED PEOPLE IN WHEELCHAIRS

5. "I don't know if I'll get elected, but boy, it sure has been good for the flour business."

—W. LEE "PAPPY" O'DANIEL, FORMER GOVERNOR OF
TEXAS AND FLOUR BUSINESS OWNER

6. "What we need is a good hurricane."

—TEXAS GOVERNOR BILL CLEMENTS, WHEN THE
IXTOCK 1 OIL SPILL DARKENED TEXAS BEACHES

7. "I am filled with humidity."

—TEXAS HOUSE SPEAKER GIB LEWIS

8. "Oh, good. Now he'll be bi-ignorant."

—TEXAS AGRICULTURE COMMISSIONER JIM HIGHTOWER,
WHEN TOLD THAT TEXAS GOVERNOR BILL CLEMENTS
HAD BEEN STUDYING SPANISH

9. "I'd just make a little bit of money, I wouldn't make a whole lot."

—TEXAS HOUSE SPEAKER GIB LEWIS DEFENDING HIM-
SELF AGAINST THE CHARGE THAT HE WOULD PERSON-
ALLY PROFIT FROM A BILL HE HAD INTRODUCED

10. "If ignorance ever goes to forty dollars a barrel, I want drillin' rights on that man's head."

—TEXAS AGRICULTURE COMMISSIONER JIM HIGHTOWER
DISCUSSING PRESIDENT GEORGE BUSH'S POLITICS

"Jake, if you'll vote fer me as County
Commissioner, I promise to fix your road
jist like I did last election!"

11. "I move we recess to go outside and throw up."

    —GIB LEWIS DURING A BUDGET HEARING

12. "Texas could get along without the United
States, but the United States cannot, except with
great hazard, exist without Texas."

    —SAM HOUSTON

13. ". . . idiots, imbeciles, aliens, the insane, and
women . . ."

—LAW STANDING IN TEXAS UNTIL 1918 REGULATING WHO
COULD NOT VOTE

14. "It's the sediment of the House that we adjourn."

    —TEXAS HOUSE SPEAKER WAYNE CLAYTON

15. "Let's do this in one foul sweep."

    —TEXAS HOUSE SPEAKER WAYNE CLAYTON

16. "The vice presidency isn't worth a pitcher of warm spit."

    —JOHN NANCE GARNER

17. "I want to thank each and every one of you for having extinguished yourselves this session."

    —TEXAS HOUSE SPEAKER GIB LEWIS

18. "We'll run it up the flagpole and see who salutes that booger."

    —TEXAS HOUSE SPEAKER GIB LEWIS

19. "It doesn't hurt 'em."

    —LBJ PICKING UP HIS PET BEAGLE BY THE EARS

# THINGS THAT MAKE YOU GO "HMMMM"

Back in the early 1950s, Richard Nixon had to face some charges of campaign irregularities which included accepting a small dog from Texas named Checkers. After going on national television to try to clear up the matter, the *Dallas Morning News* of September 24, 1952, reported in an editorial: "This country will have gotten somewhere when it demands Nixon frankness—and Nixon honesty—of every man who asks for its votes."

# ALL POLITICS IS YOKEL

**F**or reasons known only to God, Allah, Buddha, or L. Ron Hubbard, in 1986 I ran for justice of the peace in my hometown, Kerrville, Texas. Unfortunately, my fellow Kerrverts returned me to the private sector. I am not bitter. I believe that politics' loss has been literature's gain. I was mildly chagrined for a time at having lost the race to a woman but finally I offered up ninety-seven choruses of "Get Your Biscuits in the Oven (and Your Buns in the Bed)" and even graciously wrote her character into *Armadillos & Old Lace*, one of the thirteen mystery novels I've churned out—I mean carefully crafted.

As if getting beaten by a woman wasn't bad enough, one of the candidates who came in behind my second place finish chopped up his family collie with a hatchet two weeks before the election. We suspect it may have been a flashback to the Peloponnesian War. Nevertheless, he still received eight hundred votes, which gives you some idea of

> "If you elect me the first Jewish justice of the peace, I'll reduce the speed limits to 54.95!"

> "I asked the German promoter how far it was from Cologne to Paris. He thought about it for a moment and then he said: 'Oh, it's about a four-day march.' "

the mood of the electorate.

Why did Pat Knox, a woman who's not even five feet tall, beat me for J.P.? Part of the reason was that the locals reacted negatively to the five-man *Today Show* crew, headed by my friend Boyd Matson, who came down from New York to chronicle my campaign. "We're not gonna let anyone tell *us* who to vote for" seemed to be the attitude. A similar situation occurred that same year when Kurt Waldheim was elected president of Austria despite worldwide protests. This actually gave rise to a new medical condition known as Waldheimer's disease, in which you can't remember that you used to be a Nazi.

The voters did, however, really seem to appreciate my campaign slogan: "If you elect me the first Jewish justice of the peace, I'll reduce the speed limit to 54.95!"

And that, indeed, wasn't the only campaign promise I was to make during the laborious course of this tragically misguided adventure. Another pledge that went over particularly well was: "I'll keep us out of war with Fredericksburg!"

For those folks who are new to Texas or just generally cookin' on another planet, Fredericksburg is a little German town about twenty miles down the road from Kerrville where, during World War II, they tied their shoes with little Nazis. I don't want to cast asparagus upon the Germans at this time, because the German translations of my mystery books are turning out to be quite a financial pleasure for the Kinkster these days. In fact, at a book signing in Cologne, Germany, recently, I met a woman who invited me to come to Paris. I asked the German promoter how far it was from Cologne to Paris. He thought about it for a moment and then he said: "Oh, it's about a four-day march."

But it wasn't former U-boat commanders who torpedoed my candidacy for justice of the peace. It was my inability to appeal to the religious right. Still, I persevered. I even went so far as to become a Southern Baptist for a while, until I

> "I even went so far as to become a Southern Baptist for a while, until I realized that they didn't hold 'em under long enough."

> "The only downside to being a charismatic atheist, of course, is that when you die your tombstone will probably read: ALL DRESSED UP AND NO PLACE TO GO."

"Awright, we got you fer stuffin' ballot boxes
and registerin' dead people—but I admire
yore interest in politics!"

realized that they didn't hold 'em under long enough.
Today I'd no doubt be a Buddhist if it weren't for
Richard Gere.

Thus it was, because of my personal disillusion-
ment with politics and the moral decline of the
country in general, that I finally became a charismatic atheist. About the only article of faith that we
charismatic atheists truly cling to is the belief that
ballet is basketball for homosexuals. Instead of the

Four Questions tradi-
tionally asked at the
Passover Seder by peo-
ple of the Jewish per-
suasion, a charismatic
atheist asks only two ques-

> **"Today I'd no doubt be a Buddhist if it weren't for Richard Gere."**

tions. They're the same questions you're invariably
asked every time you enter a singles bar in Dallas:
"What do you do?" and "What do you drive?" The
only downside to being a charismatic atheist, of
course, is that when you die your tombstone will
probably read: ALL DRESSED UP AND NO PLACE TO GO.

But now, thanks to George W., my faith in our
political system has been restored. Not only that, but
because of George becoming president, Texas now
has its first Aggie governor, Rick Perry. For those of
you who are not blessed with being from Texas, anyone who attends or has attended A&M (Agricultural
and Mechanical) University in College Station, Texas,
is known as an Aggie. Today, of course, we like to
refer to them as Agro-Americans.

# ADVICE TO ANYONE MOVING TO TEXAS

All my adult life I've been in the practice of giving
advice to people who are happier than I am. I'm sure,
like most well-intentioned non-Texans, you're proba-

bly thrilled about moving to Texas. Now the prospect of being a Texan may make you happier than 95 percent of all dentists in America, but that doesn't mean you're going to fit in here. Remember, happiness, like Texas, is a highly transitory state. So my advice to you is the same admonition I shout every time I pass a wedding in progress: "Stop before it's too late!"

But maybe you've really set your ears back and you're hellbent and determined to become a real Texan. In that case, the least you can do is to carefully follow these few simple rules of the road for all modern Bubbas and Bubbettes. This, my fine feathered foreign friend, is friendly advice, freely given. Follow it or you get the death penalty.

1. Get you a big ol' cowboy hat and some brontosaurus foreskin boots. Always remember, the only two kinds of people who can get away with wearing their hats indoors are cowboys and Jews. Try to be one of them.

2. Get your hair fixed right. If you're male, cut it into a "mullet" (short on the sides and top, long in the back—think Billy Ray Cyrus). Or you can leave it long on top and cut it short on the sides and back. When you take off your cowboy hat you have what I like to refer to as the "Lyle Lovett Starter Kit."

   If you're female, make it as big as possible, with lots of teasing and hairspray. If you can hide a buck knife in there, you're ready.

Yep, folks, if you don't mind droughts, dust,
tornadoes, snakes, spiders and stingin'
scorpions, you're gonna love this place!

Grooming tip: If you can't find curlers big
enough, use empty Dr Pepper cans.

3. Don't make the most common mistake all non-
Texans make when they come down here—confus-
ing Amarillo with the armadillo. Amarillo is a town
in the panhandle full of people who don't like being
mistaken for armadillos. They're very conservative
politically. The armadillo is a shy, gentle creature.
It tends to be much more middle of the road.

4. Get you a big ol' pickup truck or a Cadillac. I myself drive a Yom Kippur Clipper. That's a Jewish Cadillac. Stops on a dime and it picks it up.

5. Just because you can drive on snow and ice where you come from does not mean you can drive in a Texas downpour. When it rains hard, stay home. If you have to drive, get on the highway, move into the fast lane, and go no faster than 35 m.p.h. If you have to drive at night, watch out for the deer. Only hit the ones with huge antlers because they make the best wall hanging. Christmas gift tip: Make you a nice fur coat with antlers. Give it to your mother-in-law.

6. Don't be surprised to find small plastic-sealed bags of giant dill pickles in local convenience stores.

7. If you should hear a redneck exclaim: "Hey, y'all, watch this!" stay out of his way. These are likely the last words he will ever say.

8. Remember: Y'all is singular. All y'all is plural. All y'all's is plural possessive.

9. Get used to hearing, "Hot enough for ya?" Proper response is, "Yeabuddy."

10. Don't call it "soda" or "pop." It's all "Coke" unless it's Dr Pepper.

11. Don't pet the dog standing in the back of the pickup, no matter how small or how cute. Truck dogs are all dangerous weapons. Stay clear.

12. In Texas, it is now legal to carry a concealed weapon. As a result of this recent legislation, crime has gone down. An unfortunate side effect, however, is that there are now about 18 million ambulatory time bombs any place you go, just waiting for Dustin Hoffman to pound on the hood and shout "Hey! I'm walkin' here!" As for myself, I don't carry a weapon. If anybody wants to kill me he's going to have to remember to bring his own gun.

13. Everything goes better with picante sauce. No exceptions.

14. Be sure you have a favorite football team. Be sure it is the Dallas Cowboys.

15. Don't tell us how you did it up there. Nobody cares.

## FAMOUS TEXANS NOT FROM TEXAS

**George Herbert Walker Bush:** Forty-first president of the United States, born in Milton, Massachusetts.

☆

**George Walker Bush:** Forty-third president of the United States, born in New Haven, Connecticut.

☆

**Molly Ivins:** Best-selling author and syndicated political columnist for the Fort Worth *Star-Telegram,* born in Monterey, California.

☆

**John Wayne:** Movie cowboy icon,
born in Winterset, Iowa.

☆

**Roger Staubach:** Star quarterback for the Dallas
Cowboys (1969–1979), born in Cincinnati, Ohio.

☆

**Stephen F. Austin:** Father of Texas, born in Virginia.

☆

**Jerry Jeff Walker:** Texas musician, born in
Oneonta Falls, New York

☆

**Texas Chainsaw Massacre:** Never happened in the
Lone Star State. The movie was loosely based on a
situation that occurred in Wisconsin.

☆

**Barbecue:** This well-known Texas staple was born in
South Carolina, where enslaved Haitians showed
planters how to build a framework of sticks for
smoking or roasting meat.

☆

**Kinky Friedman:** Born November 1, 1944, in
Chicago, Illinois. Lived there one year, couldn't
find work, moved to Texas. Hasn't worked since.

☆

**Slim Pickens:** Cowboy movie actor, born in
Kingsburg, California.

☆

# SEEN ON TEXAS BUMPER STICKERS

Keep Honking—I'm Reloading

☆

If You Don't Love Jesus Go to Hell

☆

God Bless John Wayne

☆

Honk If I'm an Aggie

☆

What Would Ernest Tubb Have Done?

☆

Don't Tell Mom I'm a Lawyer, She Thinks
I'm a Piano Player in a Whorehouse

☆

I Want Bush!

☆

Charlton Heston Is My President

☆

And Jesus Said unto the Mexicans:
"Don't Do Anything 'Til I Get Back."

☆

You Can Take My Gun After You Pry It
from My Cold Dead Hands!

☆

Eat More Possum

☆

I Have PMS and a Handgun

☆

Drive Friendly

☆

# HOW TEXAS GOT ITS LONE STAR

In 1821 Henry Smith became the first governor of the Mexican Province of Texas. He reportedly gave Texas its Lone Star, which is part of the official state seal.

Governor Smith wore an overcoat that had large brass buttons, as was the style of the time. It happened that the buttons on his coat had the impress of a five-pointed star. A few days after he was inaugurated governor, a messenger arrived with important papers. After reading and signing them, the governor said: "Texas should have a seal." He cut one of the big buttons from his overcoat and with sealing wax stamped the impress of the Lone Star upon the documents. So was born the Lone Star. To this day, Texas is known as the Lone Star State and her flag features one solitary white star on a field of blue, red, and white.

## ALWAYS HOLD THE DOOR FOR A LADY SHERIFF

**W**hy has Frances Kaiser of Kerr County succeeded as one of the few female sheriffs in Texas today? First of all, there's her arresting personality.

Kerr County, deep in the conservative, hunter-friendly heart of the Texas Hill Country, has long been the kind of place where Jesus could walk in with three nails and somebody'd put him up for the night. Not that it's the only place in Texas where some folks have wide open spaces between their ears, but there's no shortage of brontosaurus material. "Women votin' is bad enough," said a former deputy last seen flipping cheeseburgers at the Kerrville Burger King, "but a gal runnin' for sheriff? It ain't gonna happen in God's lifetime."

Those words were uttered long before last March, when Sheriff Frances Kaiser was effectively reelected to her third term in office after defeating ex-Texas Ranger Joe Davis in the Republican primary (she had no Democratic opponent in last month's general election).

It was also long before Governor George W. Bush had appointed her to the Texas Commission on Law Enforcement Officer Standards and Education. Today she is one of the few female sheriffs in the state of Texas. Six feet tall in cowboy boots, wearing her trademark sheriff's star earrings, the fifty-five-year-old works Winston Churchill–like eighteen-hour days beginning at six o'clock. As she told the state sheriff's convention during her first year in office, to thunderous applause, "What a great job these men have done. And I'm one of these men."

Not surprising words, actually, for someone who, though she faithfully read her Nancy Drew, has always thought of herself as "my dad's boy." Raised near Medina, the eldest of ten children born to Buddy and Nora Hubble, Frances helped take care of her five sisters and four brothers and helped her father with farm chores. Earl Buckelew, a longtime neighbor and the unofficial mayor of Medina (who, when asked about his cholesterol, said, "Hell, when we were growin' up we didn't even know we had blood"), remembers her well as a child: "Wearin' those damn ol' overalls, hair cut short—you'd see her all the time workin' the fields with her dad, bailin' hay, milkin' cows, and drivin' onto my place

> "Kerr County . . . has long been the kind of place where Jesus could walk in with three nails and somebody'd put him up for the night."

to go fishin', but I didn't mind, of course. I figured any ten-year-old girl who drives a tractor can do just about anything she wants."

> "It ain't gonna happen in God's lifetime."

And she did. In the great barefoot tomboy tradition of Amelia Earhart and Scout in *To Kill a Mockingbird*, Frances grew up strong, stubborn, and compassionate, with an occasional righteous temper that earned her the nickname Fire Eyes. Along the way, she met one of those Center Point boys, a tall, handsome marine named Richard Kaiser. She married him, had three children, drove a school bus, worked as a teacher's aide, and finally, strapping on a .357 Smith and Wesson, took to the back roads of Kerr County as its first woman patrol deputy.

When Frances thought the time had come to run for sheriff herself, her father was one of the first people she told. He didn't quite give her his blessing, but he didn't stand in her way. "I've never thought a woman should have a job like sheriff," Buddy said, "but when I look around and see the way the damn men have screwed things up, maybe it's not such a bad idea."

But certain Kerrverts, comprising a good ol' boy network carbon-dated back to australopithecine times, did not share Buddy's cautious encouragement of his daughter's political ambitions. Friends told Richard Kaiser,

> "Hell, when we were growin' up we didn't even know we had blood."
> —EARL BUCKELEW
> ON CHOLESTEROL

"You want your wife runnin' around at night? How you gonna put up with it?" And some local officials in Kerrville seemed even less enlightened. "She's just a damned woman," said a former county commissioner I last observed loading a U-Haul. "She doesn't know what she's talkin' about."

But there has never been a shortage of bubbas in this world, and even after the biblical miracle had occurred and Frances Kaiser was elected sheriff, things didn't get much easier. "If you were a man," threatened a courthouse politician shaking with rage, "I'd have handled things differently."

"How would you have handled them?" Frances asked coolly. The man sputtered, stammered, and eventually drove off in a vintage 1937 Snitmobile. And then there was the county court commissioner who, when Frances's name came up for a raise, told her, "You don't need a raise. Your husband makes a good salary."

Frances admits that her up-front style may sometimes ruffle feathers. In proving themselves in public life, she believes, women must be humble—a rather novel idea that other politicians, both men and women, might consider. "There's a way to do it," she says, "and I don't think it's to go in like gangbusters: 'By God, I'm a woman and you're damn well going to accept me.' I think it's: 'Here I am. I think I can do the job. Give me a chance.'"

Her fellow Kerrverts, of course, have given her that chance, and so far she has survived and thrived in that office for more than eight years, which is about six years longer than Suzanne Somers's television series *She's the Sheriff* lasted (but, unfortunately, a somewhat shorter life span than Suzanne Somers's Thighmaster commercials). Nonetheless, in that time the lady sheriff in the good ol' boy town has solved more cases and collared more bad guys than anybody can remember: a double-murder-suicide in which the bodies were discovered in a torched house, a triple murder featuring an elderly woman beaten to death in a wheelchair, the decapitation of a pet buffalo at a local wildlife preserve (the culprit got forty years and will eventually be hopping on a pogo stick in hell for all eternity). Not to be outdone, according to the local papers, there was the guy who O.J.'ed his wife by cutting her up into fajita-size pieces. Frances has also made one of the biggest drug busts in the history of the Hill Country and worked closely with enough cases of child abuse, substance abuse, and domestic violence to make you wonder why anybody would want to be sheriff in the first place.

> "I figured any ten-year-old girl who drives a tractor can do just about anything she wants."

> "I've never thought a woman should have a job like sheriff," Buddy said, "but when I look around and see the way the damn men have screwed things up, maybe it's not such a bad idea."

> "Jesus Christ, Frances . . . Whatever have you done to your hair?"

Aside from the normal risks and stresses of the job, on May 19, 1993, the sheriff was operated on for ovarian cancer, a circumstance that did not slow her down, although subsequent chemotherapy did force her to wear a wig to the sheriff's convention in El Paso later that year. Just as almost none of her constituents were aware of the cancer, almost none of her colleagues were aware of the wig. When the hairpiece began to irritate her while she was on a hotel elevator, she calmly reached in her purse and replaced it with a homemade turban, thus prompting a fellow sheriff from East Texas to make one of the more unintentionally humorous understatements of the year. "Jesus Christ, Frances," he said. "Whatever have you done to your hair?"

Today the sheriff appears to have triumphed over both the cancer and the good ol' boy system, though it's always possible, of course, that the good ol' boys are only in remission. She has accomplished this feat by combining a large measure of strength with a large measure of compassion. "I can handle a drunk in a fight if I have to," she says. She also says, "I believe in second chances." Both of these virtues were called front and center in late December 1994 when a local man Frances knew barricaded himself in a building in downtown Kerrville and threatened to kill himself and anybody who tried to stop him. Against all conventional procedure, she entered the building by herself. The man was as taut as piano wire, his face and features locked in a wild-eyed, shivering rictus of terror. With both hands he maintained a shooter's death grip on a .357 Magnum. Frances walked up to the man.

"Darlin'," she said. "I think you need a hug."

In the long, legendary, and sometimes lurid annals of law enforcement, this may well be the only case on record of a man turning over his gun to a Texas sheriff and receiving, in return, a hug.

> "I believe in second chances."

# RICH TEXAS OILMEN

Two rich Texans decided to take up the game of golf. Being wealthy oilmen, they hired a professional golfer to give them lessons. When the Texans showed up for the first lesson, the pro announced there would be a short delay, since there were no caddies available.

"Well, don't worry, son," said one of the Texans. "If we have to, we can use Buicks."

"Course you ain't gonna see any football players, you're watchin' the microwave!"

# TEXAS A&M FOOTBALL AND THE TWELFTH MAN TRADITION

Football has been a vital part of Texas culture since the game began. The game has been the source of many unique and noteworthy stories. The tale of Texas A&M University's "twelfth man" remains legendary for Aggies and non-Aggies alike. Non-Aggies are often amazed to see the entire student body stand throughout the entire game except during half-time. This unique Texas tradition is based on something that happened in 1922 during the "Dixie Classic" football game.

The game was played in Dallas, and A&M was facing Centre College in a hard-fought contest. The A&M team was depleted by injuries to the point that Coach Dana Bible wasn't sure he'd have enough players to complete the game. The coach remembered seeing former player E. King Gill, who was sitting in the stands; the coach had released Gill from football to play basketball earlier in the season. Coach Bible had Gill brought down from the stands and suited up on the sidelines so he would be available to play should the Aggie team need him. Gill became the team's twelfth man. The Aggies went on to win without Gill's help, but on that day a tradition was born. To this day hard-core A&M fans stand ready, as a body, to show their willingness to play if needed, to be the twelfth man.

# WRITTEN TEST FOR POLICE

The written test for the campus police at the University of Texas at Austin in the 1960s asked applicants the shape of their excrement to evaluate their ability to be observant.

# EDDIE CHILDS

When Eddie Childs was having difficulty selling his unpredictable albeit beloved Texas Rangers baseball team, he said, "I'll try to sell, but sooner or later there aren't going to be any suckers left out there."

Apparently Eddie was mistaken about that prediction. Sometime later he did sell, to a group that included the current president of the United States, George W. Bush.

# A RIDDLE

The small North Texas town of Krum boasts a citizen who is well known and beloved not only in her home state of Texas but throughout America. This celebrity is famous for her big brown eyes and loving behavior; her popularity started in 1938 and endures to this day. Who is she?

*Answer:* Elsie the cow, spokesmodel for Borden milk products.

Ain't no use agoin' to look at that pasture.
Jist sit down and watch it go by.

# YOU KNOW YOU'RE IN TEXAS WHEN . . .

You realize that anyone wearing long pants in July
is probably just visiting from Ohio.

★

Your biggest fear in the summer is tripping on
the sidewalk, falling onto the concrete, and
cooking to death.

★

You see more Texas flags flying than American flags.

★

The local paper covers national and international
news on a fourth of one page but requires ten pages
for high school football coverage.

★

You forget that rivers are actually supposed
to hold water.

★

You feel chilly when the temperature
drops below 93.

★

You notice your radiator is overheating before
you start your car.

★

You have ten favorite recipes for deer meat.

★

You put up Christmas lights when it's 90 degrees outside—at 7 A.M.

★

You can't remember life before air conditioners.

★

# TEXAS TALK

Texas talk has often confused Yankees and confounded foreigners. Words like "larruping," "blue northers," and "pole-axed" leave non-Texans scratching their heads wondering if they should sit down or get out of the way. Luckily some of the more industrious Texans have put the language to paper for outsiders to use as a guide. The following list is just a sampling of the rich language one may hear in Texas.

**"all swole up"**—This phrase is an alternative to saying one is irritated, but it can also carry connotations of being obstinate, proud, or self-absorbed.

**"blue norther"**—A storm that comes up as a giant, blue-black cloud of cold air which comes over the warm gulf air and freezes everyone to death. Rain and wind may accompany the black cloud.

**"Well, gutter my buff and call me a biscuit!"**—an affirmative comment, also used as a greeting.

**"catty whompus"**—Used to describe something that doesn't fit properly or is out of line.

**"dad blame it, dad bum it, dag nab it"**—euphemisms coined to allow expressive speech without swearing.

**"eat up"**—eaten up, destroyed, oxidized.

**"fixin' ta"**—getting ready to do something.

**"howdy"**—how do you do?

**"i-o-no"**—the Texas version of "I don't know."

**"joggerfee"**—study of the Earth's surface.

**"kin"**—relatives.

**"larrupin"**—a few fingers tastier than finger-lickin' good.

**"mona"**—used with the first person singular to state what one intends to do. Going to.

**"nut'nduin"**—means I will not, would not, could not, or should not do that.

**"over yonder"**—directional phrase meaning "over there."

**"pole-axed"**—knocked flat, smashed flat with dramatic force.

**"Q"**—never pronounced by a Texan. Instead, KW is used. Example: "kwane," which refers to the king's wife.

**"rot"**—the opposite of left.

**"shoot"**—an expletive.

**"turd floater"**—a very heavy downpour.

**"u-betcha"**—an affirmative comment, normally used alone. Example: "Didja get paid today?"

**"whole nuther thing"**—something else entirely.

**"yawl"**—collective second person singular. Also spelled "y'all."

**"zat"**—replaces the two words "is that." Example: "Zat your dawg?"

# THE TRAIN TRACK CHILDREN

There is a story in San Antonio about a school bus in which a number of children were killed in a train wreck. The bus had stopped and stalled on the middle of the train tracks in the southeast part of town. The train came, hit the bus, and killed the children. Since then, many people have gone to the site. Visitors park their car on one side of the railroad tracks, place it in neutral and then claim to feel it pushed by ghostly little hands across the tracks to safety. Some visitors wash their car before going and then sprinkle baby powder on the back of the car. According to the stories, after the car is pushed across the tracks, little handprints are left in the powder. Every year, particularly at certain times of the year, more and more people are taken to the location and claim to witness this phenomenon for themselves. The spot was even featured on several television shows investigating the supernatural.

# COMING OF AGE
# IN TEXAS

Looking at the stars in the Texas sky you couldn't tell the difference between now and then. But it's there, all right. It's the difference between a picture you carry in your wallet and a picture you carry in your heart. But hearts can be broken and wallets can be stolen and you know you've grown up when you realize how far you are away from the stars.

In the early 1950s, however, when I was a child, I spat as a child, I shat as a child, and I wore a funny little pointed birthday hat as a child. I knew what every little kid knows about Indians which in a purely spiritual sense can often be considerable, and of course absolutely nothing about ex-wives. When I grew up and was finally released from the Bandera, Texas, Home for the Bewildered for rhyming words too frequently, I knew a little more about Indians and still absolutely nothing about ex-wives except what Alden Shuman had once told me: "They'll stick with you through thick."

> **"They'll stick with you through thick."**

As far as Indians go, which is usually a good bit farther than ex-wives, I've collected about a million arrowheads over the years and made frequent visits to the Frontier Times Museum in Bandera, which is just down the street from the Bandera Home for the Bewildered. As well as countless Indian artifacts, the museum features a real shrunken head, a two-headed goat, and many other weird and arcane objects that delighted me as a child and, because of a rather unfortunate state of arrested development, continue to hold the same fascination for me now.

Children, it has always seemed to me, have a greater inherent understanding of many things than adults. As they grow up, this native sensitivity is smothered, buried, or destroyed like someone pouring concrete over cobblestones, and finally replaced by what we call knowledge. Knowledge, according to Albert Einstein, who spent a lot of time, incidentally, living with the Indians when he wasn't busy forgetting his bicycle in Princeton, New Jersey, is a vastly inferior commodity when compared with imagination. Imagination, of course, is the money of childhood. This is why it is no surprise that little children have a better understanding than most adults of Indians, nature, death, God, animals, the universe, and some truly hard-to-grasp concepts, like the Catholic Church.

Now, with the eyes of a child, I lit my first cigar of the morning and focused softly on everything that wasn't there. I'd survived half a century on this primitive planet where the pecking of poison parakeets in the Northern Territory of Australia was the very least of our worries. I cast my mind back to when I was seven years old, sitting like Otis Redding on the dock at the deep water at Echo Hill Ranch in the Texas summertime. It was there and then that a rather seminal experience occurred in my young life, a small thing actually, but as Raymond Chandler often observed in his final stages of alcoholism: "Tiny steps for tiny feet." It was the first time I'd ever seen a man's testicle, unknowingly suspended, almost like a Blakean symbol, outside the lining of his 1950s-style bathing suit.

The man was named Danny Rosenthal, a nice man with a moustache and a cheery smile who probably had his own problems then, but, of course, as a child, these were not known to me. Danny Rosenthal was a friend of my father's, and the only problem that I could see that he had at the moment was that a singular large, adult testicle was trapped like a dead rat outside the lining of his bathing suit. Danny Rosenthal was totally oblivious of this, but it delighted me as a

> **"Imagination, of course, is the money of childhood."**

child, and because of a rather unfortunate state of arrested sexual development, continues to hold the same fascination for me now. Danny Rosenthal's testicle, indeed, hangs suspended like a sun over the happy memories of the last days in the lifetime of my childhood.

You don't see people's testicles hanging out of their bathing suits much anymore. Styles have changed, people have changed, the world's a different kind of place, they say. Instead of looking up at things we now spend most of our time looking down on them. Another reason we don't have Danny Rosenthal's testicle to kick around anymore is that people don't appear to have any balls these days. Balls, like imagination, seem to shrivel with age.

As far as Danny Rosenthal is concerned, I believe I remember my father saying that he stepped on a rainbow some years back. If that is indeed the case, I'm sure he's now swimming in the sky with his wayward testicle relegated in the way of all flesh to the shadows on the walls of Hiroshima. I've never told anyone about this small incident of a small child, least of all Danny Rosenthal, but I'm sure he's long past the mortal stage in which social embarrassment might have been incurred. I believe God watches over every testicle, even those that

> "Instead of looking up at things we now spend most of our time looking down on them."

sometimes, quite invol-
untarily, stray from the
herd. I believe that all of
us will some day be
swimming in the sky
with Danny Rosenthal,
or at least wind up in a

> **"I believe God watches over every testicle, even those that sometimes, quite involuntarily, stray from the herd."**

bar somewhere singing Jimmy Buffet cover songs.

## MORE HOMETOWN HEROES

1. Tommy Tune — Wichita Falls
2. Larry McMurtry — Archer City
3. Dan Blocker — O'Donnell
4. John Nance Garner — Detroit, Texas
   (Thirty-second vice president of the United States, under FDR)
5. Jayne Mansfield — San Antonio
6. Waylon Jennings — Littlefield
7. Nolan Ryan — Alvin
8. George Jones — Saratoga
9. Dennis Quaid — Houston
10. Jerry Hall — Mesquite
11. Larry Hagman — Fort Worth
12. Carol Burnett — San Antonio
13. Scott Joplin — Linden

14. Gene Roddenberry,          El Paso
    *Star Trek*

15. Huddie Ledbetter           Navasota
    (wrote "Goodnight Irene")

16. Dale Evans                 Uvalde

17. Sandra Day O'Connor        El Paso

18. Wiley Post                 Grand Saline

19. Audie Murphy               Kingston

20. Spanky "Our Gang"          Fort Worth
    McFarland

# HOW TO SPOT A TEXAN ABROAD
(anywhere outside the Republic of Texas)

If her hair has ever gotten hit by the ceiling fan:
TEXAN.

If his pickup has an umbrella in the shotgun rack:
NOT A TEXAN.

If he wears his Wranglers with one pants leg
tucked in his boot and the other out: TEXAN.

If the Jeep he just bought is a two-wheel drive
automatic: NOT A TEXAN.

"I guess this means you won't be open today!"

If her makeup was applied with a spackling tool:
TEXAN.

★

If she orders tea in a restaurant and assumes it's
going to be anything other than iced: NOT A
TEXAN.

★

If he lists high school football as his religion:
TEXAN.

★

If she doesn't own a teasing comb and hair spray:
NOT A TEXAN.

★

If he prefaces every name with "Old" (example:
"Old Earl is going to drop by later on"): TEXAN.

★

If she can't chew gum and smoke a cigarette at the
same time: NOT A TEXAN.

★

If he gets teary-eyed and sentimental when
describing his first gun: TEXAN.

★

If none of their children have ever shot a gun
before: NOT TEXANS.

★

If the first day of hunting season is a school holiday for their children: TEXANS.

★

If they find stuffed animal heads mounted on the
wall distasteful: NOT TEXANS.

★

If they know more than two people named
"Skeeter": TEXANS.
(Bonus points if a person's own name is Skeeter.)

★

If they don't pull over to the side of the road when
a funeral procession is anywhere in sight: NOT
TEXANS.

★

If they spend more than three minutes talking about BBQ sauce: TEXANS.

★

If they never heard the phrase "Hot enough for ya?": NOT TEXANS.

★

If their favorite bar has sand or sawdust on the dance floor and Willie Nelson songs on the jukebox: TEXANS.

★

If he takes his cowboy hat off indoors: NOT A TEXAN.

★

# ARMADILLO FAST FACT FILE

An armadillo always gives birth to four identical young—the only mammal known to do so. All four young develop from the same egg and share the same placenta.

Armadillos will dig a burrow as long as fifteen feet in which to bear their young.

Armadillos are used in leprosy research because their body temperature is low enough for them to contract the most virulent form of the disease.

Female armadillos are capable of "virgin birth." This is a result of the female's ability to delay implantation of the fertilized egg during times of stress. This reproductive strategy is one reason why 'dillos are so good at colonizing new areas.

Armadillos come out only when it is very cloudy, late in the afternoon, or at nightfall. This is because their eyes are very sensitive to light.

Armadillos like to swim, and they are very good swimmers. They have a strong dog paddle and can even go quite a distance underwater, walking along the bottom of streams and ponds. When they need to float, they gulp air into their intestines to make them more buoyant.

Armadillos have a very long, sticky tongue to eat insects as quickly as possible. They also are equipped with strong claws to tear open ant nests. An armadillo can eat over 40,000 ants in one sitting.

Armadillos have a very low metabolic rate, which means that they don't waste a lot of energy producing heat. But it also means that they are not well adapted to living in cold areas, because they can't keep warm very well. They do not have any fat reserves, so they must forage for food on a daily basis. Just a few cold days in a row can be deadly to an armadillo.

One way armadillos conserve energy is through a *reta mirabila* (Latin for "miraculous net"), a system of veins and arteries in their legs. Not much heat actually goes out into the legs; thus it is kept in the body. Armadillos get frostbitten very easily, since they have no way to warm their extremities through blood flow.

Baby armadillos have soft shells, like human fingernails. The shells get harder as the animal grows, depositing bone under the skin to make a solid shell.

Somewhere in the universe there is a planet inhabited principally by sentient armadillos who occasionally carve up dead humans and sell them as baskets by the roadside.

# PRISONER-OF-WAR CAMPS IN TEXAS

During World War II, there were more than seventy prisoner-of-war camps in Texas, easily more than in any other state. Primarily housing German soldiers from the famed Afrika Korps, the camps in Texas also held Italian and Japanese prisoners. Certain German prisoners of war somewhat affectionately called the armadillo "Panzer Swine."

# DIGGING THE ROOTS OF TEXAS MUSIC

*"Cadillacs were getting longer, and dreams were getting as close as they ever do to coming true."*

The past and the present, I've always thought, are very deeply intertwined. History is what happens when one of them gets a little ahead of the other. This is probably why inspiration is often borrowed in the strangest ways from other places and other times.

Before they were moptops, the Beatles cut their hair like Tony Curtis and took their name from the Lubbock, Texas, band, the Crickets. One of the Beatles' earliest, funkiest, most primitive-sounding demos reportedly was a cover of "That'll Be the Day," which was never released and remained "lost" over the years like a pearl in the snow. Recently, the original demo was sold at Sotheby's to an unknown buyer for a price supposedly in the neighborhood of $40,000. Possibly a Japanese insurance company or someone with the soul of a Japanese insurance company.

> "Before they were mop-tops, the Beatles cut their hair like Tony Curtis and took their name from the Lubbock, Texas, band, the Crickets."

The demo itself may no longer be important, but its reason for existing in the first place tells us something vital about the deep, gnarly, long-reaching roots of rock 'n' roll. And it tells us something about the spirit of a time and a place far away. The song was written by the young Buddy Holly immediately after seeing a John Wayne movie.

They say Texas is a state of mind, and maybe it is. The Texas tradition of music is so deep and multilayered it would require seven archaeologists with seven brooms seven years just to clear away the dust. When they got to the bottom, after digging through village upon village, they'd probably find king of Western swing Bob Wills's cigar lying next to blues legend Mance Lipscomb's guitar.

As a true Texas Jewboy, I recall growing up in the early 1950s, a bastard child of twin cultures. Later I observed some similarities as the two ways of life melded into my own. The songs of both groups, it seemed, were invariably heartfelt, and the music was always of the traveling variety. I realized that cowboys and Jewboys were both wandering—very possibly vanishing—Gypsies of the soul, and whether you light campfires or candles as you walk the torturous trail of this world, nobody really

"Gosh, Slim, shorley you boys wouldn't want me
to take a chance on hurtin' my guitar-pickin'
finger choppin' that ol' cedar!"

gives a damn whether you make it to the last
roundup.

Musically and culturally speaking, the 1950s in
Texas were insular in many ways. When the decade
was dawning, even Willie Nelson, who would
become a symbol of Texas and much of its musical
legacy by the 1970s, couldn't find anyone willing to
give him a tumble.

"In 1950, I was seventeen years old, fresh out of

"**Texas is a state of mind.**"

high school," Nelson says. "A quick, miserable eight months in the U.S. Air Force and then back to Texas to restart my music career. On the way through the 1950s in Texas, I sold cars and books in Fort Worth, where I was fired as a singer in a North Side bar because I wasn't commercial. I guess you could say the 1950s in Texas were noncommercial for me."

But eventually Texas did become a financial pleasure for Nelson, and because of Texas, so did the rest of the world. Maybe it's because Texas provided physical and spiritual elbow room.

Texas's size and fierce independence of spirit often seem to produce an achingly vibrant expanse of time and geography, out of which it is sometimes possible to dream a little bigger. This is not only true for Willie Nelson; it is the only way the Buddy Hollys of this planet are born.

Buddy Holly grew up in the Panhandle of Texas in a simpler time. Cadillacs were getting longer, tail fins were getting higher, dreams were getting as close as they ever do to coming true. It was an era of boom and innocence. As Kent Perkins, an old friend of mine, observed: "Man had not discovered the moon, but he had discovered the moon pie." And nobody remembered where they were the day Kennedy was shot. Buddy Holly was a child of his times.

Sonny Curtis, a member of the Crickets (and possibly the only American to have his songs recorded by both Bing Crosby and the Dead Kennedys), remembers that Holly had a wide appreciation of all musical forms, from bluegrass to early blues stylings by blacks. Curtis first met Holly in Lubbock, Texas, in 1951 and has vivid memories of staying up half the night in Buddy's car, listening to *Stan's Record Rack*, a blues program out of Shreveport, Louisiana. Holly's love of early black music is obvious. He recorded "Rip It Up," by Little Richard, and "Brown-Eyed Handsome Man," by Chuck Berry, and often sang Ray Charles's songs, including "I Got a Woman," and "This Little Girl of Mine."

In 1956, Curtis went to Lubbock's Cotton Club to see the blues piano player Charles Brown and remembers being "the only white face in the place." Ironically enough, in early 1957, when Buddy Holly and the Crickets played the Apollo Theater, in Harlem, they were the only white group on the program because of a mix-up by the promoter, who thought they were black. The crowd didn't mind, however. The audience loved them.

> "I realized that cowboys and Jewboys were both wandering—very possibly vanishing—Gypsies of the soul, and whether you light campfires or candles as you walk the torturous trail of this world, nobody really gives a damn whether you make it to the last roundup."

> "Cadillacs were getting longer . . . dreams were getting as close as they ever do to coming true."

Holly's harmonies also show a clear bluegrass influence. According to Curtis, Holly once tried unsuccessfully to copy Earl Scruggs's stylings with just a flat pick and a four-string banjo. But two things happened in 1955 that turned Holly's head around. One was meeting Bob Wills at the Clover Club, in Amarillo; the other was when Elvis Presley came through Lubbock.

Curtis remembers that Elvis wore red pants, an orange jacket, and white bucks, and Holly and Curtis—both around seventeen at the time— thought that was about the coolest thing they'd ever seen. The two of them had opened the show on January 2, 1955, so they had backstage privileges, which included talking to Elvis and "getting right up in his face." Elvis had recorded "That's All Right (Mama)" on Sun Records, and Holly was already a big fan. Curtis also recalls that cotton bales were set up all around the stage and police were posted to keep women from attacking Elvis. Presley got paid seventy-five dollars for the show, which he split with Bill Black, his bass player, and Scotty Moore, his guitar player. The day after the show, according to Curtis, he and Holly started "playing Elvis full tilt."

Holly was into leather work at the time, and

Curtis remembers Buddy making a beautiful wallet trimmed in pink and black with ELVIS in pink letters. A year and a half later, driving through Memphis on the way to Nashville, Holly dropped the wallet off for Elvis at Sun Records. By then, of course, Elvis wasn't using wallets. He was using wheelbarrows.

Sonny Curtis's recollections effectively evoke the pure innocence and exuberance of rock 'n' roll of the times. "We used to rehearse in Holly's garage because they had an old empty butane tank in there, and we'd get a great echo from it," Curtis says of Holly's first band in high school. "We were so excited. It was almost like something was looming in the future."

The Pulitzer Prize–winning writer Larry McMurtry remembers the 1950s in Texas as "a dying twinge of depression—gray, dust-blown, intolerant." Ray Benson of Asleep at the Wheel recalls that Texas was "heaven, although hotter than hell the summer of 1958 to an eight-year-old Yankee who loved Roy Rogers, Tex Ritter, and all singing cowboys." Larry King, the playwright who wrote *The Best Little Whorehouse in Texas,* remembers the times as being "super-reactionary, segregationist, and mean." I remember taking jitterbug lessons in Houston,

> "Man had not discovered the moon, but he had discovered the moon pie."
>
> —KENT PERKINS

> "Blues and country are the same thing, just the moods are different. It all comes from life experiences."
>
> —HUEY P. MEAUX

Texas, from a girl named Susan Kaufman.

Maybe all of us were right. But one thing is sure: At the beginning of the decade, the black music and the white music were almost as completely separate as the segregated communities from which they came. With time, radio, the borrowing of inspiration, stylings and good looks, and the help of undaunted early musical pioneers, the cultures grew together in the dusty laboratory of life into a wild, highly contagious new strain of music called rock 'n' roll.

Huey P. Meaux, the legendary Houston record producer, saw no reason for the separation. He remembers blacks and whites crossing the tracks, picking cotton together, singing together in the fields, then going home their separate ways. He recalls sitting in the swamps as a child, getting eaten alive by mosquitoes, listening to black people playing blues. That was as close as the times would let him get.

"Blues and country are the same thing," says Meaux, "just the moods are different. It all comes from life experiences." The early bluesmen were real, he believes; they bucked the system, they "couldn't care less if the Russians invaded today or tomorrow."

This attitude was later adopted by the rockers of the 1960s, who widened the scope a bit: They didn't care if the Martians invaded today or tomorrow.

Along with Alan Freed and Phil Spector, Meaux experimented with what was at the time labeled "mix-breeding music." All three suffered for it, Meaux contends, but he adds that they eventually "broke a hole through the clouds." It didn't make much sense that Jimmy Reed, Chuck Berry, Fats Domino, and Little Richard played mostly to white people and that T-Bone Walker, Percy Mayfield, Charles Brown, and Big Mama Thorton played mostly for blacks. Why not widen the audience as much as possible?

The Big Bopper, J. P. Richardson, was the first disc jockey in Texas to play a mixed-format show; it was so hot that nobody could touch his ratings with a barge pole. "The blue-chip white cats hated it," Meaux says of the show on Beaumont's KTRM and the changes it helped produce, "but black and white kids were going to the sock hops together."

Meaux remembers the Big Bopper, who recorded for Mercury, getting ready for a session. They were all convinced that "The Purple People Eater Meets the Witch Doctor" was going to be a big hit, but the record needed a backside. Forty-eight

> "He cried a song and it was a feeling you couldn't forget. He had teardrops in his voice."
> —HUEY P. MEAUX

> **"Old blues cats never sang the same song the same way twice."**
> —HUEY P. MEAUX

hours before the session, Richardson wrote "Chantilly Lace." It was one of the first major commercial successes of black vocal stylings performed by a white artist.

Blacks were also beginning to embrace a different kind of music. Just a week before Buddy Holly first saw Elvis Presley, the R&B crooner Johnny Ace lost his last game of Russian roulette. It happened backstage on Christmas Day at Houston's Civic Auditorium, where the singer was appearing. Ace's death remains rather mysterious, and many say that he was murdered. The twenty-five-year-old Ace had a huge hit song at the time, "Pledging My Love."

According to Meaux, "Johnny Ace was the first black guy I know of, way before Ray Charles, who could sing country-tainted songs—blues and country together. He cried a song, and it was a feeling you couldn't forget. He had teardrops in his voice."

The cross-pollination wasn't limited to Texas: Imagine a line stretching from San Antonio to Baton Rouge to Macon, Georgia. Below that line is an area that has consistently turned out artists who appeal to both black and white listeners. The reason, Meaux says, is that every fifty to a hundred miles there was a little enclave of Czechs, Bohemians, Poles, Mexicans, or Cajuns who played Polish polkas, Mexican polkas, Cajun two-steps, boleros, waltzes, *conjunto,* and many other unique musical forms.

"In those days," says Meaux, "you had to learn to play different towns with different nationalities and musical stylings." The singer and accordionist Clifton Chenier, whom Meaux produced, helped effect a special kind of musical hybrid, combining black and Cajun-style music to create what is now zydeco.

Black music and the blues have had so much influence on the world that if you look at the whole cloth of today's music, the black threads almost seem to hold the tapestry together. Those black threads go all the way back to the old bluesmen.

Some lacked education and couldn't write down the lyrics, some often forgot them, and some probably liked to give the guys who were following them around with tape recorders a hard time. But one fact Huey P. Meaux knows for sure: "Old blues cats never sang the same song the same way twice."

Back in the 1950s, the hard-shell Southern Baptists used to pull down their window shades when they were hosing, so nobody'd

Hank Williams played in San Antonio on his last birthday, September 17, 1952. "He had the number one song in the country, 'Jambalaya,' and was paid five hundred dollars."

think they were dancing. We had religion in Texas in those days, but as far as I can remember, nobody was born again. Most of us figured it'd been tedious enough the first time around.

But there are many ways of "seeing the light" in this world, and one of them has always been through country music. Hank Williams's death, on January 1, 1953, struck a muted, lingering chord across the South. Williams was only twenty-nine when he died: younger than Jesus and Mozart. He wasn't born in Texas, but his music will always live there. Maybe there's something in the dust and the dreams and the distance of Texas that has helped Williams's music carry across the years. His last hit became a cultural anthem for the people on the lost highway of the 1950s. It was "I'll Never Get Out of This World Alive."

There were other voices of the times, though, other stars in the Texas sky—Bob Wills and the Texas Playboys, Ernest Tubb, Hank Thompson, and Charlie Walker, to name a few. In 1958, Walker, a boyhood hero of mine, had the big country hit "Pick Me Up On Your Way Down."

"In the early 1950s," Walker told me, "I had

> "Hank Williams's death, on January 1, 1953, struck a muted, lingering chord across the South. Williams was only twenty-nine when he died: younger than Jesus and Mozart."

a country-music club, the Old Barn, in San Antonio. Hank Williams played for me there on his last birthday, September 17, 1952. He had the number one song in the country, 'Jam-

> "The 1950s in Texas may not have been the Paris of the 1920s, but how many different kinds of sauces can you put on a chicken-fried steak?"

balaya,' and was paid five hundred dollars."

The roots of some of today's most enduring country musicians in Texas easily reach back to the 1950s and further. Billy Joe Shaver and Jerry Jeff Walker seem to have an almost karmic linkage with the storytelling singing cowboy. Ray Benson and Asleep at the Wheel have made new generations aware of the great tradition of the Western swing bands that once dominated the Southwestern musical landscape. The keyboardist Augie Meyer, who played with Doug Sahm, derived his style from Spanish country music, which features the accordion and the *vayo sexto*, a Spanish guitar fitted with twelve piano strings.

These distinctive styles nevertheless fall under the heading of country, and the country-music boom in the 1950s enriched them all. If country music truly stems from life experiences, then the 1950s were vividly real, undecaffeinated times. The 1950s in Texas may not have been the Paris of the 1920s, but how many different kinds of sauces can you put on a chicken-fried steak?

"Longevity has ruined as many men as it's made."
—WILL ROGERS

In the end, all that seems to survive is the music. Where it originated, what influenced it, and how it was passed along, we can't always know for sure. But we do know that before the Beatles started listening to the Crickets, and before Huey P. Meaux and a few other brave souls began messing with the music and the minds of so many different kinds of people, still earlier instances of "mix breeding" had occurred.

One such incident took place around 1935 and involved a twelve-year-old boy who would go further than he dreamed and a man named Tee-tot. Tee-tot was a black blues singer who literally sang for his supper, and on the streets of Greenville, Alabama, he taught Hank Williams how to play the guitar.

If Williams's death brought the 1950s in with a dull, gray morning, Buddy Holly's plane crash over Clear Lake, Iowa, on February 3, 1959, was the other spiritual bookend for the decade. What Buddy Holly, Hank Williams, Johnny Ace, or, for that matter, Mozart and Jesus might've become had they lived is something about which we can only speculate. As Will Rogers once remarked: "Longevity has ruined as many men as it's made."

Some things change, and some things remain the same, and some you always seem to miss the first time around so you're never sure what happened to them. "Hell, in the 1940s we were still riding horses to school," says Larry King, "but by the 1960s we'd be riding, stoned, in new cars on new freeways." The saying, "Don't spit on the floor" that graced the wall inside the Medina, Texas, post office disappeared sometime in the late 1950s. There are still occasional signs saying WE RESERVE THE RIGHT TO REFUSE SERVICE TO ANYONE  in little out-of-the-way greasy spoons around Texas, but they hang rather forlornly and mostly just gather cobwebs these days. And the oldest Methodist church in Kerrville has had the cross lopped off the top of it and an aluminum drive-through window installed and is now a savings and loan. Now *that's* progress.

You'll be pleased to know, however, that according to the Kerrville Bus Company's posted regulations, it is still prohibited to transport bull semen by bus.

> "Hell, in the 1940s
> we were still riding horses
> to school, but by the
> 1960s we'd be riding,
> stoned, in new cars on
> new freeways."
> —LARRY KING

Yes, I believe there is a little disagreement
over the judgin'!

## STRANGE TEXAS LAWS

When two trains meet each other at a
railroad crossing, each shall come to a
full stop, and neither shall proceed
until the other has gone.

✸

It is illegal to take more than three sips
of beer at a time while standing.

★

You can be legally married by publicly
introducing a person as your husband or
wife three times.

★

It is illegal to milk another person's cow.

★

A recently passed anticrime law
requires criminals to give their victims
twenty-four hour notice, either orally
or in writing, and to explain the nature
of the crime to be committed.

★

The entire *Encyclopedia Britannica*
was once banned in Texas, because
it contained a formula for making
beer at home.

★

In Abilene, it is illegal to idle or loiter
anyplace within the corporate limits
of the city for the purpose of
flirting or mashing.

★

In Lubbock County, it is illegal to drive
within an arm's length of alcohol—including
alcohol in someone else's bloodstream.

★

In Mesquite, it is illegal for children to have
unusual haircuts.

★

In Port Arthur, obnoxious odors may not
be emitted in an elevator.

★

In San Antonio, it is illegal for both sexes
to flirt or respond to flirtation using the eyes,
the hands, or both.

★

It is illegal to urinate on the Alamo.

★

# FINAL MEAL REQUESTS
# BY TEXAS DEATH ROW INMATES

Stacey Lawton: (executed 11/14/00)
1 jar of dill pickles.

★

Cornelius Goss:  (executed 2/23/00)
1 apple, 1 orange, 1 banana, 1 coconut, peaches.

★

Miguel Flores:
3 beef enchiladas w/ onions, 3 cheese enchiladas
w/ onions, Spanish rice, bowl of jalapeños, french
fries, cheeseburger all the way, bowl of ketchup,
bowl of pico de gallo, 3 Dr Peppers, pitcher of ice,
banana split, 4 quesadillas.

★

William Kitchens: (executed 5/9/00)
6 sunny-side-up fried eggs, 8 pieces of pan
sausage, 6 slices of toast w/ butter and grape jelly,
crispy hash browns, milk, and orange juice.

★

Frank McFarland: (executed 4/29/98)
Heaping portion of lettuce, a sliced tomato, a
sliced cucumber, 4 celery stalks, 4 sticks of
American or Cheddar cheese, 2 bananas, 2 cold
half-pints of milk. Asked that all vegetables be
washed prior to serving. Also asked that the
cheese sticks be clean.

★

Jeffery Allen Barney: (executed 4/16/86)
2 boxes of frosted flakes, 1 pint of milk.

★

Charles Rumbaugh: (executed 9/11/85)
1 flour tortilla, a glass of water.

★

Robert Streetman: (executed 1/7/88)
2 dozen scrambled eggs, flour tortillas,
french fries, ketchup.

★

Jonathan Nobles: (executed 10/7/98)
Eucharist, Sacrament.

★

Carlos Santana: (executed 3/23/93)
Justice, tempered with mercy.

★

# TEXAS MURDERERS

Colonel Colt, Winchester Arms, and early Texas didn't see all the relatively senseless killings in Texas history. The following is a short list of Texas murderers, with the number of their victims.

1. Kenneth McDuff      12+

2. Bonnie and Clyde      14

3. John Wesley Hardin      39

4. Richard Speck      8
   (His victims were all student nurses.)

5. George Jo Hennard      23
   (His victims were dining at the Luby's
   in Killeen when they were murdered.)

6. Charles Whitman      18
   (His victims were his wife, his mother,
   and 16 students.)

7. Yolanda Saldivar      1
   (killed the Tejano singing star Selena while
   serving as president of her fan club)

8. Henry Lee Lucas      200+
   (Lucas later denied killing that many.
   He was eventually executed.)

9. Charles "Tex" Watson        5 1/2

(5 victims plus Sharon Tate's unborn baby)

10. Lee Harvey Oswald        1

(killed one president, winged a governor)

"I'll represent dern near anybody, but I draw the line at a man fool enough to steal cows on a bum market in the middle of a drought!"

## MAY ALL YOUR JURIES BE WELL-HUNG

In Texas they say Racehorse Haynes can get a charge of sodomy reduced to following too closely. It may sound like something of a Texas brag, but there's no doubt that this man has the raw human power to demolish a stone-faced courtroom jury like Judy Garland on a good night.

On this particular balmy May night in Houston I enter Haynes's River Oaks mansion and find Racehorse's wife, Naomi, (whom Racehorse refers to as "the widow Haynes") and a group of friends sitting in the living room watching television. Racehorse himself is not there, but Naomi points the way and I wander through the cavernous place until I come to a small study, the door of which is open. I enter and find Racehorse Haynes, arguably the greatest criminal lawyer in the world, sitting at his desk, puffing his pipe with the Zen-like dedication of Inspector Maigret, and reading a large tome of Cicero. Haynes graciously gets me a chair and a little liquor drink for the heat, and I ask him why, like most other good Americans, he isn't watching television instead of reading Cicero.

> "In Texas they say
> Racehorse Haynes can
> get a charge of sodomy
> reduced to following
> too closely."

"Read the classics one hour every day, drunk or sober," says Haynes. "Reading the classics gives one a feeling of confidence. It familiarizes one with the vagaries of life. It shows one that there are really no new plots."

Every so often Haynes stops to clean or tamp his pipe with an object he fondly refers to as "state's exhibit one"—a large, rather sinister-looking knife that figured in a homicide. The original owner of the knife, Haynes's client, had made a date with another man, spent a lot of time primping for it, and then got stood up when the other man decided to go home to his wife. The defendant, whom Haynes sometimes calls "my guy," then drove over to the man's house in a 1948 snit.

"The deceased was killed by his homosexual lover," says Haynes, "while the man's wife was watching."

"And he got off?" I ask. Haynes nods.

"He's now a productive member of society."

"Because you got him off," I say. I take a few righteous puffs on my cigar and Haynes takes what appear to be several thoughtful puffs on his pipe.

Then he speaks in a quiet but forceful voice. "I don't get people off," he says. "The jury acquits them."

I take a slug of my drink and Haynes goes back to futzing with his pipe and the murder weapon formerly belonging to the alleged homosexual killer. Haynes catches me looking at the knife and suddenly smiles an incredibly warm and disarming smile.

"It doesn't make the *knife* evil," he says. "It's a good knife."

Richard "Racehorse" Haynes was born sixty-three years ago in Houston, Texas, to a family so poor that at age two he had to be shipped off to San Antonio to live with his grandmother. His granny was a little over four feet tall, drank a pint of gin a day, and taught young Richard so well that he was able to fill out the forms himself at school in order to bypass the first and second grades. Back in Houston, Haynes went to junior high, where he picked up the name "Racehorse" from a disgruntled football coach. In two consecutive plays, Haynes was unable to break through the line, so he headed rapidly for the sidelines, thereby racking up fifty yards without advancing the ball. "Goddamn! What do you think you are?" said the coach. "A racehorse?"

On February 19, 1945, at the age of sixteen, one beach or so to the right of Ira Hayes, Racehorse Haynes fought with the U.S. Marines at Iwo Jima. He was missing for twenty-six days, but he was one of the few who lived to tell about it.

My eye wanders over to the glass case near the door of Haynes's study. It is filled with a collection of toy soldiers large enough to give pause to General Patton.

"When I was a kid, I didn't have any toy soldiers," says Haynes. "Not any store-bought toy soldiers."

Haynes's life is a rags-to-riches story. In 1938, in front of a movie theater where he sometimes saw cowboy movies for a nickel, Haynes was arrested by a juvenile officer for writing his initials in the wet concrete. Fifty-three years later, along with Dan Rather, Dr. Denton Cooley, and others, Haynes was asked to write his name again and record his footprints in cement in front of the same movie house, as part of the "Heights Walk of Honor," a celebration of the neighborhood's hundredth birthday.

Haynes has been known to do whatever it takes, within the law, including drinking a glass of Ortho-Sevin pesticide, shocking himself repeatedly with an electric cattle prod, and, legend has it, damn near halfway crucifying himself on a tree in order to prove his client's innocence. Possibly the most dangerous thing Haynes ever did, however, was in

> "Read the classics one hour every day, drunk or sober," says Haynes. "Reading the classics gives one a feeling of confidence. It familiarizes one with the vagaries of life. It shows one that there are really no new plots."

the late 1940s when, with
a tractor-like extension,
he drove a Ford convert-
ible from Fort Worth to
Houston while sitting in
the backseat and steering

> **"I don't get people off,"
> he says. "The jury
> acquits them."**

with his feet. He did that just for the hell of it.

Racehorse contends that the guilty are sometimes in more need of the help the law can provide
than are the innocent. I ask him if he's always sure
his client is telling him the truth.

"I've been conned a couple of times in thirty-five
years," he says. "I've spent a lot of time thinking
Humpty-Dumpty was pushed. But I can't prove it."

As our conversation winds its way through murder and mayhem, I mention the Rodney King case,
in which twelve of LA's finest whipped up rather
severely on one black motorist. This leads logically
to an earlier, somewhat similar case of Racehorse's.
In that case, two white Houston cops, one of whom
was a martial arts expert, had been charged with
kicking a black man to death, the coroner having
allegedly located the deceased's liver in about seven
different counties. Haynes, representing the cops,
moved successfully for a change of venue to New
Braunfels, a little German town in the Texas Hill
Country not particularly known for its progressive
mores. Haynes himself is no redneck, not even a
good ol' boy. In spirit, he seems to be closer to

> **"I've spent a lot of time thinking Humpty-Dumpty was pushed. But I can't prove it."**

Atticus Finch in *To Kill a Mockingbird*. He's a lawyer for the damned, and he believes strongly in "representing people, not things." But he will do whatever it takes within the law to defend his client—so meanwhile, back in New Braunfels . . .

"There were some black college kids from Houston who'd driven up to protest the trial," says Haynes. "The local sheriff comes up to me in the courtroom and tells me about it. 'We stopped 'em,' he says. 'Thirteen carloads of niggers. We locked 'em up in the jail.' 'You can't do that,' I told him. 'They haven't broken any law.' 'They sure the hell have,' says the sheriff. 'They had gambling paraphernalia. We found a deck of cards in one of the cars.' 'Good thinking, Sheriff,' I told him. 'That's really using your ol' elbow.'"

The two white cops were acquitted. Says Haynes: "The jury chose to believe that the black man slipped on a rock while attempting to evade capture."

But probably the most interesting, revealing, and humorous thing about the whole affair occurred after the trial was over, when a reporter approached Haynes in a local bar. Haynes contends that he did not know that the man was a reporter. Nonetheless, the exchange was widely reported in the state press.

"Racehorse," said the reporter, "when did you know that the case was won?"

"When they seated the twelfth U-boat commander in the jury box," said Haynes.

Because Racehorse is a busy American and I didn't want him to start charging me his usual rate (estimated at over $1,000 an hour, and that was before inflation), I let him out to pasture for the rest of the evening. We parted on fairly cordial terms with Haynes promising to take me to his secret weapons locker over the weekend, and aboard his fifty-two-foot yacht. "The yacht's called *Integrity*," he says with a smile. "For people who say I don't have any."

You have to use a lot of allegedlies and a lot of reportedlies when you write about Racehorse Haynes, but in between the two you find a good, possibly great, and modest man who still does ten percent of his work on a pro bono basis, sort of as a tithe. He continues this practice even today, although he was report-edly paid over six-teen million dollars once for a single case—that of T. Cullen Davis, the wealthiest man in history ever to be brought up on a murder charge. Haynes didn't get him

> "You run the car over the witness, look back over your shoulder for signs of life, run the car back over him, and then park the car over his grave."

> "One thing you look for just before the verdict," says Berg, "is a laughing or smiling jury. That's always a good sign."

off either, of course. The jury acquitted him.

To get a fresh angle on Racehorse, I drive a few blocks and stop before the posh River Oaks mansion of another big-time criminal lawyer, David Berg, known to intimates in the profession as the "Silver Bullet." I'm feeling vaguely like Lieutenant Columbo as I enter the huge place, which is lit up like a Christmas tree in Las Vegas.

"You have to understand that a man's reputation is a delicate thing," says Berg. "So anything I say about Racehorse Haynes is with great admiration and the fervent hope that he'll croak and all his clients will call me."

I mention the nickname, "Silver Bullet," about which Racehorse has already confided: "Berg can't pay people to call him that." Berg says: "Haynes doesn't want me to have a nickname because he thinks I'll make more money than he does." Berg, a longtime friend and protégé of Racehorse's, seems almost as good a source for material about Haynes as the man himself. Berg describes their style of cross-examination as follows: "You run the car over the witness, look back over your shoulder for signs of life, run the car back over him, and then park the car over his grave."

Berg describes one of Racehorse's "Smith and Wesson divorce" cases where Haynes represented a wife who paid a hired killer to have her husband "dusted." "One thing you look for just before the verdict," says Berg, "is a laughing or smiling jury. That's always a good sign. But in this particular case of Haynes's, when the jury room was opened, there sat twelve people all holding hands and praying. When Haynes saw that he turned a whiter shade of pale. But you never know what a jury will do, especially after a closing argument from Racehorse. The jury acquitted the woman of murder. As Haynes himself often says: 'One thing a trial lawyer never has to worry about is constipation.'"

Berg tells also of the first time he saw Haynes. The Silver Bullet had just won his first courtroom case. The year was 1970, Berg was a young radical civil rights lawyer, and the case was before the U.S. Supreme Court. When he entered a crowded lawyer's convocation in a Houston hotel ballroom the following week, he was shunned like a leper for his civil rights stand and his brash success. As he was taking a seat in a corner, wishing he could disappear, he looked up at the podium and saw Racehorse Haynes addressing the conference. Haynes paused in his prepared remarks, looked over at the far corner, and said: "Congratulations, Lawyer Berg." Haynes began to applaud and soon the whole ball-

> **"One thing a trial lawyer never has to worry about is constipation."**

room joined him. The Silver Bullet was on his way.

The following afternoon Haynes and I are skimming silently along in his dark blue Rolls Royce Corniche through the rain-swept streets of downtown Houston. We are en route to what must remain the undisclosed location of his secret weapons locker. Haynes is telling me about the time several years ago when Norman Mailer came to Houston to discuss doing a book about Racehorse's life. The two of them got along very well, and Mailer developed an additional interest in Haynes when he learned that the lawyer had once been a welterweight Golden Gloves champ. The two of them were in the lobby of the Westin Galleria Hotel with about a hundred people watching when Mailer suddenly struck a stance and began slap-boxing with Haynes. The slap-boxing degenerated, as it usually does, until the two of them were slapping each other pretty hard and the crowd had swelled to a fairly respectable gate. At that point, according to Haynes, he stopped, removed his wrist-watch, and handed it to Mailer to hold for a moment. Mailer put forward both hands to hold the watch and Haynes slapped him a good one in the face.

"Not everything slick happens in Brooklyn," he told Mailer.

It is Sunday morning, and most Americans are in worshipful attendance at the Church of the Latter Day Businessman as the Silver Bullet and I speed toward the Lakewood Yacht Club to join Racehorse aboard the *Integrity*. David Berg is telling me a bit more about Haynes's courtroom style, which might safely be described as Clarence Darrow meets Jimmy Swaggart with little dollops from time to time of Jesus Christ and Loretta Young for Cajun seasoning.

Berg contends that Racehorse never will chastise a witness for a belligerent or bullshit answer. According to Berg, Haynes will say something like: "Perhaps it was the way I asked my question." Then, as the cross-examination proceeds, blaming the lack of understanding upon himself, he'll persistently repeat the sentence, subtly changing the inflection. "Perhaps it was the *way* I asked my question . . . Perhaps it was the way I *asked* my question."

"Soon," says Berg, "the guy starts talking with Haynes, gets into a rhythm with him, trying to outsmart him. That's the guy's mistake. Haynes leaves the witness like a pane of glass dropped from a thirteen-story building, with jagged shards all over the floor of the courtroom."

**"Not everything slick happens in Brooklyn."**

The Silver Bullet entertains me on the rest of the way out to the yacht club with some of the gory details of a case Berg handled in 1982. A father and his twenty-eight-year-old son were arguing about Earl Campbell's contract with the Houston Oilers. The father, like every good Texan, had a gun nearby, and proceeded to blow his son's head off.

"We take our football seriously here in Texas," I say.

"The story does have a happy ending," says the Silver Bullet. "He was acquitted."

"There's always the chance that justice will be done," says Racehorse, as he leads the way into the Lakewood Yacht Club dining room with Berg and myself in tow. In my high rodeo drag, I don't look as though I belong in anybody's yacht club, but since we're with Racehorse, we attract only a few cool, next-door-to-civil stares. Racehorse is mildly amused.

"I did much better a few months ago," he says, "when the widow Haynes and I brought a black lady in here."

> "Haynes leaves the witness like a pane of glass dropped from a thirteen-story building, with jagged shards all over the floor of the courtroom."

Over dinner and drinks, Berg mentions a client that Racehorse had successfully defended recently. The client was grateful to have been acquitted but was complaining about what he saw as an exorbitant fee. "This isn't criminal law," the client had said, "It's estate planning."

Haynes laughs at the comment. "The accused is entitled to a speedy trial," he says, "but not necessarily a fast one."

> "The judge declared 'not guilty,' I shook hands with my guy and told him he could thank the jury if he wished. So he stands up and he says to the jury: 'Thank you. I'll never do it again.'"

Haynes, the first in his family ever to go to college, tells us that at one time he was a premed student who found himself constantly cutting classes to watch Percy Foreman try cases. Then he visited several hospitals. "Room after room of the smells and the pain of sickness and death and no one could really do anything about it." Haynes stares into some long-ago middle distance. Then he says, almost to himself: "As a lawyer, at least I can appeal."

"Criminal lawyers must be like the brain surgeons of the legal profession," I say.

"No," says Haynes quickly. "We're the bastard stepchildren of the profession. Nobody likes us until they need us."

Over Key lime pie, Racehorse explains why he seldom if ever allows clients to take the stand for themselves, or indeed, to say anything at all to the court. In general, most people are uncomfortable in the courtroom setting, and so they may appear stilted or unnatural to a jury and thereby jeopardize their own case. But Haynes, as a younger lawyer, had a personal experience in court that militates against his ever normally letting a defendant speak for himself.

"I believed my guy was innocent and, apparently, the jury agreed," says Haynes. "So when the bailiff handed the verdict to the judge and the judge declared 'not guilty,' I shook hands with my guy and told him he could thank the jury if he wished. So he stands up and he says to the jury: 'Thank you. I'll never do it again.'"

Later in the afternoon, aboard the *Integrity*, it's beginning to sound a little like a Texas tall tales convention, with the only difference being that everything that is said is true, most of it documented by court records. Haynes, relaxing behind the helm, is describing his infamous "outlaws' crucifixion case" in which he defended Fat Frank, Super Squirrel, Crazy John, Mangey, and other members of a biker gang who stood accused of crucifying a lady on a tree. The bikers were in the habit of urinating and spitting on their jackets before they put them on, wearing dead rats on their lapels, and French kissing each other every time they met in public. They did this, so they said, according to Racehorse, "to break people's minds so they'd leave our ass alone." Haynes appears to vaguely empathize with the sentiment, if not the methodology.

This "lady," it appears, was somewhat proud of the crucifixion, because, unlike Jesus and Spartacus, to name only two, she survived to wear the nails on her leather jacket

> **"Berg's argument for a change of venue was that only the feet were found in Harris County. The knees and legs were in Nueces County, the buttocks in El Paso, the hips and lower abdomen in Arizona, and the shoulders and head in California."**

and show off her stigmata at local bars. Haynes did his best to get the bikers ready for the trial.

"I showered 'em down," he says, "and told them not to French kiss in the courtroom. Unfortunately, Fat Frank hadn't seen one of his buddies in a long time and, sure enough, there they went."

Haynes's recounting of the crucifixion case goads the Silver Bullet into a rather lurid evocation of his famous "five easy pieces case," which he once described to the *New York Times* as "pretty brutal, even for Texas."

"It was one of the earliest battered-wife defenses," says Berg. "A woman took a hacksaw and cut her husband up into five pieces, but what the jury found a little hard to swallow was when she went back to the hardware store for a second blade."

> **"A woman took a hacksaw and cut her husband up into five pieces, but what the jury found a little hard to swallow was when she went back to the hardware store for a second blade."**

Haynes laughs. "It was artful lawyering," he says. "Berg's argument for a change of venue was that only the feet were found in Harris County. The knees and legs were in Nueces County, the buttocks in El Paso, the hips and lower abdomen in Arizona, and the shoulders and head in California."

"She was acquitted," the Silver Bullet adds needlessly.

Racehorse, after some badgering from the crew, rises to the occasion with several more insider's angles on well-known cases. It's now fairly clear, according to Haynes, that Dr. John Hill, thought by many to have killed his wife by poisoning an eclair with *E. coli* bacteria, was innocent as Racehorse maintained. The wife's symptoms, now seen in the pale light of the modern era, more plainly resemble toxic shock syndrome, which was unknown at the time of the trial.

During the infamous "Kerrville slave ranch trial," Haynes did indeed shock himself several times with an electric cattle prod one afternoon in front of hundreds of local Kerrverts on the courthouse lawn. "It hurt," he now says, "but it wasn't lethal." The father and son team who allegedly tortured a drifter to death with the device (their homemade tape recordings of the torture sessions were played at the trial) can now be seen dining fairly regularly at the Kerrville McDonald's.

Cullen Davis, who is now an evangelical preacher, allegedly killed his stepdaughter and shot and wounded his wife in 1976 in his six-million-dollar mansion on 148 acres near downtown Fort Worth. Witnesses testified that after being shot through the middle with a .38, Davis's wife walked half a mile, called the hospital, and later that night performed fellatio on the doctor in the operating room.

"She was a very durable lady," says Racehorse.

The doctor steadfastly refused to talk and, according to Haynes, "if he was the recipient of this hospital kindness," it might have had some bearing on the case, but now, "the answer to the question may be lost to the world." Davis himself claimed he was in a movie theater at the time of the shooting, as a party of one, watching *The Bad News Bears*.

I asked Haynes and Berg what irons they have in the fire that they can tell us about. Is there some special case that each may be currently looking to put his brand on?

> **"When he ran for governor of Texas, Adams reportedly listed his occupation as 'alleged white-collar criminal.'"**

"Berg is still taking victory laps," says Haynes, "for that railroad case of his in Angleton."

Berg, who is one of the few lawyers in the country to score big verdicts in both criminal and civil cases, takes over the figurative helm.

"It was a wrongful death case," says the Silver Bullet, "in which a black woman was killed at a railroad crossing in a small town in South Texas called Angleton. During the course of the trial, one of the attorneys for the railroad was allegedly overheard to have remarked: 'No nigger's going to get any money in Angleton, Texas.' In April of this year the jury brought in a verdict of twelve and a half million dollars for the family of the woman."

Racehorse is keeping pretty much to the inside track with information about the big case he'll be taking to trial soon in Austin, Texas. The details he does mention sound like a story out of *Star Trek* with a sidecar of James Bond. It is a savings and loan case in which Haynes will defend a man named Stanley Adams who, incidentally, is the first person to register for ownership of an S&L on the moon.

> **"The gravitational pull of the CIA is so intense that everything that goes into it disappears. Even light cannot escape from it."**

The government will be trying to show that Adams did a somewhat less than adequate job of running an S&L right here on earth with the

Lamar Savings and Loan in Austin, Texas. Adams, in fact, should prove an interesting challenge for Racehorse as a client. In the past, when he ran for governor of Texas, Adams reportedly listed his occupation as "alleged white-collar criminal."

"The government," says Haynes, "won't be able to show that Adams took money out of the S&L and put it in his pocket. Instead, he took money out of his pocket to keep his dream alive."

I ask Racehorse if it's true, as the Silver Bullet avers, that "former officers of S&L's are wading ankle-deep in both of their offices."

Haynes laughs, then becomes more serious. "I see a dark thread of CIA mischief in this case," he says. "Mysterious transactions of mysterious men with mysterious connections with that most mysterious arm of our government. I hope the CIA will march forward like little men and confess, but that's a pipe dream. They don't even confess to the Congress of the United States."

Racehorse puffs on his pipe and ponders going head to head with the CIA. "It's the 'black hole theory,'" he says. "The gravitational pull of the CIA is so intense that everything that goes into it disappears. Even light cannot escape from it."

Then he looks over the bow at the darkening sea and smiles a winning smile that is, in almost measurably equal parts, manly confidence and boyish mischief. "We're gonna try to light a candle in there," he says.

As the landing party comes ashore, the last image I have is of Racehorse Haynes standing alone on the *Integrity*. There is a thoughtful silence in the air, almost as if we've all been listening to some famous magical closing argument. It is the words, the substance, the voice, the gestures, the style of a man who loves what he does and does it better than almost anyone else on earth.

The Silver Bullet and I don't speak until we're on the road back to Houston. Then he says: "Racehorse is not doing God's work—he's defending the Constitution. The people who think they're doing God's work in this country are the ones who wind up in the electric chair."

Late that night as I drive toward the Texas Hill Country, I think of all the colorful, exciting, big-time cases Haynes has handled in a lifetime in court, with lives at stake and fortunes on the line. Then I remember a case he'd told me about the first time we talked in the little study in the big mansion. It was a trial that had taken place in the late 1950s. It received almost no publicity and he'd received no fee for his work. Yet, according to Haynes, it still remains closest to his heart.

Haynes was defending a black man who stood accused of theft of construction materials, a charge Haynes felt was clearly a frame-up. When a verdict of "not guilty" was brought in, the man, his 250-pound wife, and a half a dozen of his children all ran to the middle of the courtroom, jumping up and down and hugging Haynes.

> "Racehorse is not doing God's work—he's defending the Constitution. The people who think they're doing God's work in this country are the ones who wind up in the electric chair."

That night he was invited to a little party out in the ghetto. It was a shotgun-railroad house like the kind put up by the company store. The man and his wife were there, all the kids, the old grandma. There was barbecue and soda pop. And on the walls, the kids had taken crayons and written: "God Bless You, Mr. Racehorse."

Wul, we're gonna have to breed shorter-legged cattle
or start a-fixin' fence.

## TEXAS IS THE ONLY STATE

Texas is the only state in the union that entered as a
republic and retained its right to become its own
country again and divide itself up into five states.
This ability to divide has been brought up at various
times over the years when Texans are not happy with
the way the country is being run.

# TALL TALES

Three cowboys are sitting around a campfire, out on a lonesome Texas prairie, each full of the Texas pride for which cowboys are famous. A night of tall tales begins.

The first one says, "I must be the meanest, toughest cowboy there is. Why, just the other day a bull got loose in the corral and trampled ten men to death before I wrestled it to the ground by the horns with my bare hands."

The second cowboy refuses to be bettered. "Hell, that ain't nothing. I was walking to the saloon yesterday and a twenty-foot rattlesnake slid out from nowhere and coiled up to strike me. I grabbed that snake with my bare hands, bit its head off and sucked the poison down in one gulp. And I'll be damned if I ain't still here today."

The two cowboys looked toward their friend and waited for his story. The third cowboy remained quiet, however, as he silently stirred the coals with his penis.

# FAMOUS TEXANS WITH MUTANT GENITALIA

1. John Wayne Bobbitt: His wife Lorena amputated his penis while he slept and later threw it out the window of her car. A hawkeyed policeman recovered the organ and doctors were able to successfully reattach it. Mr. Bobbitt went on to perform in adult videos before he disappeared into obscurity. (Ed. note: John Wayne Bobbitt is not a Texan by birth. He is, however, Kinky insists, a Texan by inspiration.)

2. Mr. Lifto: A performer in the Jim Rose Circus sideshow. During the show he performs the following feats of strength: lifts 75 pounds with his pierced penis (his penis sports a piercing the thickness of a little finger); lifts 125 pounds with his pierced nipples; lifts a car battery with his pierced tongue.

# HISTORY OF DR PEPPER

In the year 1885, an English pharmacist named Charles Alderton was working at the Morrison's Old Drug Store in Waco, Texas. He also experimented with mixing various carbonated soft drinks together and tasting them. When he happened upon a combination that appealed to him, he offered his boss, Wade Morrison, a taste, and Morrison was also deeply impressed.

The drink became very popular among customers having a treat at the soda fountain in the drugstore. Mr. Morrison decided to name the drink after the man who had given him his first job back in Virginia years before: Dr. Charles Pepper.

The drink became so popular that other drugstores in the area began to buy it from Alderton and Morrison, until the Old Drug Store was unable to produce enough to satisfy the demand.

The solution was soon found in the person of a man named S. H. Prim, who owned a bottling plant in Dublin, Texas. This plant still exists today and uses the original recipe, bottled with 100 percent pure cane sugar.

But a young beverage chemist, the owner of the Circle "A" Ginger Ale Company, is the man responsible for introducing the United States' first major soft drink to the masses. Robert S. Lazenby and Morrison formed a partnership in which Morrison would give Lazenby the formula and trademarks in exchange for providing bottling facilities, labor, and distribution. Alderton wasn't interested in being a partner, and Prim also turned down an offer for a franchise of his choice in 1922.

In 1904, Lazenby and his son-in-law J. B. O'Hara introduced Dr Pepper to approximately twenty million people at the World's Fair Exposition in Saint Louis. Interestingly enough, this same fair had introduced buns for hot dogs and burgers earlier, and also the ice cream cone.

The soft drink was a hit, and Morrison and Lazenby officially formed the Artesian Mfg. & Bottling Company. They moved the company to Dallas in 1923, and then changed the name a year later to the Dr Pepper Company. By 1946, the company was listed on the New York Stock Exchange and in 1950 the period was dropped after the Dr.

In the early 1910s Dr Pepper was advertised as the "King of Beverages." In the 1920s and 1930s it had a logo: "Old Doc," an old country doctor with a top hat and a monocle. A slogan at this time was "Drink a Bite to Eat at 10, 2, and 4." New research had shown that people's energy level dropped around 10:00 A.M., 2:00 P.M., and 4:00 P.M. and the Dr Pepper Company used this information as a marketing tool, suggesting that the drink would raise one's energy level. In the 1950s Dr Pepper was advertised as "The Friendly Pepper Upper." The advertisement of the 1960s was "The Most Misunderstood Soft Drink," and the one in the 1970s was "The Most Original Soft Drink in the World."

In 1977 the slogan was "Be a Pepper." Many of us in our thirties and older remember this jingle—"I

Drink Dr Pepper and I'm Proud. I'm Part of an Original Crowd . . . Be a Pepper, Drink Dr Pepper." The slogan in the 1980s was "Hold out for the Out of the Ordinary" and the newest slogan in the year 2000 was "Dr Pepper Makes the World Taste Better."

Extra trivia: Dr Pepper was the first major soft drink introduced in the United States, followed by Coke and then Pepsi.

# AGGIE JOKES

What do you call a smart person on the A&M campus?

Answer: A visitor.

The Texas equivalent of a Polish joke is an Aggie joke. No one knows how the practice started, but it has gone on for years and has become as much a part of Texan culture as longhorn cattle. In fact, some of the best Aggie jokes come from Texas A&M students and alumni.

Many Aggie students hang signs outside their rooms encouraging their team to beat the hell out of their next opponent. A year or so ago, when no game was scheduled, the sign read "Beat the hell out of Open Date!"

Then there was the Aggie who took a correspondence course during the summer. One day he decided to go fishing instead of completing his lesson, so he sent in an empty envelope. It's the only time in history anyone ever cut class in a correspondence course.

At a recent Longhorn versus Aggie football game, someone fired a gun in the stands. The Longhorns, thinking time had expired, left the field. But the Aggies continued to play. Seven plays later, they scored.

Did you hear about the Aggie who locked his keys in the car and it took him three days to get his date out? That same Aggie was riding in the back of a pickup truck that suddenly went out of control and off a bridge into a lake. The poor Aggie drowned because he couldn't get out of the pickup—the tailgate wouldn't open.

Two Aggies were holding up a flagpole and doing their best to measure it, without much success. A stranger happened along and suggested that if they laid the pole down on the ground, it would be easier to measure. "That won't work," said one of the Aggies. "We want to know how tall it is, not how long."

Two Aggies were walking down the street and they met the local rabbi with his arm in a cast. "What happened to your arm, Rabbi?" one of them asked. "I slipped in the bathtub and broke it," said the rabbi. The first Aggie turned to the second Aggie and asked: "What's a bathtub?" The second Aggie said: "How do I know? I'm not Jewish."

And then there was the Aggie who moved to Oklahoma and raised the intelligence levels of both states.

"Now this is called cleanin' up
in the cow business!"

# LITTLE-KNOWN FACTS ABOUT THE ALAMO AND HER DEFENDERS

More than 2.5 million people a year visit the 4.2-acre complex known worldwide as "The Alamo." On March 6, 1836, the Alamo fell to General Santa Anna's Mexican army. The death of the Alamo defenders has come to symbolize courage and sacrifice for the cause of liberty. Below are some facts not widely known about the Alamo and her defenders:

1. William Travis's slave Joe was one of two defenders who survived the battle of the Alamo.

2. The Alamo was of no military importance at the time. Its significance was symbolic and psychological. Santa Anna's goals were political, not military, and he believed that soundly defeating the rebels in the Alamo would cause the sensation he was after. His main fear was that Travis would surrender before an attack could be mounted.

3. One of the Tejano defenders had a brother in Santa Anna's army. Gregorio Esparza was the only Alamo defender who was allowed to be buried in a separate, marked grave; his brother Francisco obtained permission from General Cos to recover Gregorio's body. Gregorio's wife and children survived the battle.

4. After the Battle of the Alamo, the Texans killed by Santa Anna's army were taken by carts to what is now East Commerce Street. There they were stacked like kindling and set ablaze. The bodies burned for two days and the skies over San Antonio were darkened with thousands of vultures.

5. William Travis, commander of the Alamo, kept a diary of, among other things, all his sexual conquests and their ordinal number in his love life.

Bonus fact: It is illegal to urinate on the Alamo. The heavy metal artist Ozzy Osborne urinated on the Alamo and was blackballed from ever performing in San Antonio again.

## *THE ALAMO:* JOHN WAYNE'S CLASSIC MOVIE

John Wayne had originally wanted to film *The Alamo* in Durango, Mexico, but that location was nixed when prominent Texans let it be known that they wouldn't permit the film to be distributed in Texas if it were shot in Mexico. The film was shot in Bracketville, Texas, instead.

☆

It took two years to build the set for *The Alamo.*

☆

*The Alamo* was the most expensive movie in motion picture history up to that point.

☆

The movie was banned in Mexico.

☆

# AFTER THE ALAMO

It is said that after Santa Anna surrendered to Texans after the battle of San Jacinto, he was brought before Sam Houston, who was to decide the Mexican general's fate. The Battle of the Alamo was still fresh in the minds of the Texans, and they wanted to execute Santa Anna. At one point, the Mexican general gave Sam Houston a secret handshake. Houston, a well-known Mason, quickly recognized the handshake as the secret Masonic sign of distress. Brother Masons are bound by honor and tradition to respond when they are given the sign. Sam Houston spared the general's life, much to the dismay of his vengeful men.

Later, Santa Anna claimed to be in pain and asked for some of Houston's "painkillers." Houston obliged; he and his captive sat around and smoked opium, then later drew up the plans for the annexation of Texas.

# THE TEXAS CHICKEN RANCH

The famous historic bordello known as the Chicken Ranch was located in La Grange. The roots of this rural whorehouse can be traced back to 1844. It operated for part of its 130-year history under the protection of a local law official.

The "house of sin" was operated by a madam called "Miss Edna." Edna Milton came to the ranch in 1952. This Texas institution, known for being a place of initiation into manhood for Texas A&M freshmen, was closed in 1973 as a result of an exposé by a Houston TV newsman, Marvin Zindler. The exposé generated so much publicity that it became the inspiration for a movie and a Broadway play, written by Larry L. King, entitled *The Best Little Whorehouse in Texas.*

"Hey! Where you goin' with my dog!"

# STRANGE SPORTS MASCOTS IN TEXAS

**The Hutto Hippos:** Hutto High School.
According to a legend, the Hippo was adopted
as the Hutto High mascot because of a
hippopotamus that had escaped from a circus
traveling through Austin. The hippo was
eventually found in a creek near Hutto.

★

**Horned Frogs:** Texas Christian University
takes its mascot name from the increasingly
scarce insectivorous lizard that looks like
a miniature holdover from prehistoric days.

★

**Polar Bears:** Frost High School,
in a Central Texas town, chose this name
in spite of the fact that the town had had only
two inches of snow in twenty years.

★

**Buttons:** Central Catholic High School,
San Antonio, Texas. A "button" is the name
for a baby rattlesnake. This mascot is appropriate
because Central Catholic served as a "feeder"
school to a local university, St. Mary's, that uses
the mascot name "the Rattlers."

★

**Wampus Cats:** Itasca High School.

This mythical creature can take any one of a
number of manifestations, from fierce to comical.
At times a rumor will arise that an actual wampus
cat has been caught or spotted. A wampus cat is a
six-legged blue cat that looks like a mountain lion.
The local newspaper stated the reason for the six
legs: "Four to run at the speed of light.
Two to fight with all its might."

★

**Cottonpickers:** Robstown High School.

The school is located in South Texas—or the
"Valley" as it is also known—a place where almost
anything grows, including cotton. At one time, many
of the people in this area were employed in the pro-
duction of cotton. Now machines do most of the
work of picking cotton, but the people of the area
still take pride in being known as "Cottonpickers."
The name of the school's gym is the "Cotton Gin."
At one point, the school actually had someone dress
as a cotton ball. When that person graduated,
no other student would step up and assume
this awesome responsibility.

★

**Fighting Farmers:** Lewisville High School.

The town's main water tower is emblazened
with a picture of a football player running with a
pitchfork aimed straight ahead.

★

"Shore, I'm a cowboy . . . saw
Willie Nelson one time!"

# THE BACK OF
# THE BUS

**I** met Willie Nelson on the gangplank of Noah's
ark. Like most country music friendships, ours
has managed to remain close because we've stayed the
hell away from each other. I've played a few of Willie's
picnics and we've attended the same Tupperware par-
ties now and then, but, ironically, I didn't really
start feeling spiritually akin to him until I'd phased
out of country music almost entirely and become a
pointy-headed intellectual mystery writer. Now that
my novel, *Roadkill*, features Willie as a main character, our karma is suddenly linked—whether we
like it or not.

Even when Willie produced a record of mine in
Nashville in 1974 (and sang backup with Waylon
Jennings and Tompall Glaser on "They Ain't Makin'
Jews Like Jesus Anymore"), he and I were still close
enough only for country dancin'. Of course, we'd
come from different backgrounds. Willie had picked
cotton in the fields as a kid in Abbott. For income
from local farmers, he'd go out with a little home-

made paddle and kill bumblebees; he would come home looking as if he'd just fought fifteen rounds with God. Willie grew up never having much money or much schooling and got married and divorced about ninety-seven times. All he ever wanted to do was write songs and sing them for people and maybe get one of those cars that roared down the highway with the windows rolled up in the middle of summer, indicating that the driver could afford that ultimate symbol of success: air conditioning.

By the time Willie finally got that car, it was about ten minutes too late to make any difference, but he did get something else far more important: He got a bus. In fact, he got three buses. The one he lives in and calls home is known as the Honeysuckle Rose. The way I first really got to know Willie was by traveling with him aboard the Honeysuckle Rose. It's a floating city unto itself, with "floating" the operative word. Even the secondhand smoke has been known to make casual visitors mildly amphibious. (There is no truth, incidentally, to the widely held belief that Willie needs the other two buses to carry all the weed he smokes on the first bus.) By contrast, my own country music career never quite reached the tour-bus level. The closest I came was a

> "Like most country music friendships, ours has managed to remain close because we've stayed the hell away from each other."

blue Beauville van, out of which the Texas Jew-boys poured like a thousand clowns at every honky-tonk, minstrel show, whorehouse, bar, and bar mitzvah throughout the South, to paraphrase Jerry Jeff Walker. The Beauville,

> "There is no truth, incidentally, to the widely held belief that Willie needs the other two buses to carry all the weed he smokes on the first bus."

like my career, was not a vehicle destined for vastly commercial country music stardom, though it did have at least one good quality: It broke down in all the right places.

Also unlike Willie, I came from an upper-middle-class home, which is always a hard cross for a country singer to bear. I got a guitar as a young teenager in Houston, and like Townes Van Zandt, the song I first learned was "Fraülein." By then Willie and his sister, Bobbie, were already playing in beer halls on Saturday nights and in church the next morning. By the time I had my bar mitzvah, Willie had sold Bibles and written "Family Bible," which he also sold, reportedly for $50.

Willie never went to college, but I graduated from the University of Texas's highly advanced Plan II liberal arts program, which was mainly distinguished by the fact that every student had some form of facial tic. Then I joined the Peace Corps and worked in the jungles of Borneo, while Willie con-

> "By the time I had my bar mitzvah, Willie had sold Bibles and written 'Family Bible' which he also sold, reportedly for $50."

tinued writing, singing, marrying, divorcing, struggling, and smoking. As I said, I don't really know what Willie and I have in common—other than the fact that we're both pretty fair bumblebee fighters. Probably it has to do with what Johnny Gimble, the great country fiddler, told me once aboard the Honeysuckle Rose. He said that when he was a kid he'd told his mother, "Mama, when I grow up, I'm gonna be a musician." His mother had answered, "Make up your mind, son, because you can't do both."

If Willie had been Rosa Parks, there never would have been a civil rights movement in this country, because he refuses to leave his soulful locus at the back of the bus unless it's to go onstage or onto a golf course. Golf is a passion with Willie, and it's the one aspect of his life I find stultifyingly dull. As I once told Willie, "The only two good balls I ever hit was when I stepped on the garden rake." Willie, of course, responded to this news with a golf anecdote. He told me about a woman who'd recently come off his golf course at Briarcliff, went into the pro shop, and complained to the golf pro that she'd been stung by a bee. "Where'd it sting you?" asked the pro. "Between the first and second holes," she

said. "Well I can tell you right now," said the golf
pro, "your stance is too wide."

After I had written a number of mystery novels
and traveled extensively with Willie, the idea crossed
my dusty desk to write a book with him as a central
character, set the scene aboard the Honeysuckle
Rose, and let the bus take the story wherever the hell
it went. This meant I would be exchanging my New
York loft with the cat and the lesbian dance class
above for Willie and his crew. Willie had never been
a character in a murder mystery, but he thought it
might be worth a shot, so to speak.

We crisscrossed the country together. As the song
goes: "Cowboys Are Frequently Secretly Fond of
Each Other." Willie sang, played chess, and smoked
enough dope to make him so high that he had to call
NASA to find his head. As for myself, I smoked
cigars, drank a little Chateau de Catpiss, played chess
with Willie, and wrote down many things at all hours
of the day and night in my
little private investiga-
tor's notebook. Along the
way, I went to many of
Willie's shows. Wandering
around backstage at a
Willie Nelson concert is
a bit like being the par-
rot on the shoulder of the
guy who's running the

> "Mama, when I grow up,
> I'm gonna be a musician."
> "Make up your mind, son,
> because you can't do both."
> —LEGENDARY FIDDLE-
> PLAYER JOHNNY GIMBLE
> AND HIS MOTHER

> "If Willie had been Rosa Parks, there never would have been a civil rights movement in this country, because he refuses to leave the back of the bus."

Ferris wheel. It's not the best seat in the house, but you see enough lights, action, people, and confusion to make you wonder if anybody knows what the hell's going on. If you're sitting out in front, of course, it all rolls along as smoothly as a German train schedule, but as Willie, like any great magician, would be the first to point out, the real show is never in the center ring. As Willie always says, "Fortunately, we're not in control."

Backstage has its similarities at any show, whether it's Broadway or the circus or the meanest little honky-tonk in Nacogdoches—the palpable sense of people out there somewhere in the darkness waiting for your performance, or being able to pull a curtain back slightly and experience the actual sight of the audience sitting there waiting to be entertained by someone who, in this case, happens to be you. It's the reason Richard Burton vomited before almost every live performance of his life. It's part of the reason George Jones took Early Times, Judy Garland took bluebirds, and many a shining star burned out too soon. Standing alone in the spotlight, up on the high wire without a net, is something Willie Nelson has had to deal with for most of his adult life.

One night at Billy Bob's in Fort Worth, I was standing backstage in the near darkness when a voice right behind me almost caused me to drop my cigar into my Dr Pepper. It was Willie. "Let me show you something," he said, and he pulled a curtain back, revealing a cranked-up crowd beginning to get drunk, beginning to grow restless, and packed in tighter than smoked oysters in Hong Kong. Viewed from our hidden angle, they were a strangely intimidating sight, yet Willie took them in almost like a walk in the trailer park.

"That's where the real show is," he said.

"If that's where the real show is," I said, "I want my money back."

"Do you realize," Willie continued in a soft, soothing, serious voice, "that ninety-nine percent of those people are not with their true first choice?"

He looked out at the crowd for a moment or two longer. Then he let the curtain drop from his hand, sending us back into twilight.

"That's why they play the jukebox," he said.

Willie's character leaped off the stage and onto the page. I don't know if you'd call it Jewish radar or cowboy intuition, but during my travels with Willie, a story line began to evolve. He would be at the center of one of my

> "Cowboys are frequently secretly fond of each other."
>
> —NED SUBLETTE

> **"Of John Wayne, he once said, 'He couldn't sing and his horse was never smart.'"**

most challenging cases. There wasn't a butler to do it, but Willie did have a valet named Ben Dorsey, who'd once been John Wayne's valet. This provided some humorous commentary, since Willie wasn't an enormous fan of the Duke's. Willie preferred the old singing cowboys. Of John Wayne, he once said, "He couldn't sing and his horse was never smart." (That kind of talk never failed to irritate Dorsey and usually resulted in some sort of tension convention.) Other real characters who inhabit the Honeysuckle Rose and the pages of *Roadkill* are Bobbie Nelson, Willie's sister; Lana Nelson, Willie's daughter; Gates "Gator" Moore, his intrepid bus driver; L. G., his one-man security team; and a cast of thousands of friends, fans, and family, who, along with life itself, did everything they could to interrupt our chess games.

You can tell a lot about a man by his chess game, unless, of course, your opponent is smoking a joint the size of a large kosher salami. Edgar Allan Poe once said of chess: "It is complex without being profound," and it is because of that very complexity that a momentary loss of concentration or the entry of some foreign emotion, like a broken heart, can torpedo the game. When you take this into consideration, Willie plays with the evenness of the Mahatma, at a lightning pace, and rarely loses. (I, of course, rarely lose either.)

One of the things I admire most about the way Willie plays the game of chess, as well as the game of life, is his Zen Texan approach to inevitable triumphs and defeats. The endgame doesn't hold great interest for him, because he's already thinking about the next game. If he comes off less than his best in one game, one show, one interview, one album, his next effort is invariably brilliant. This is one of the reasons I've always looked up to both Willie Nelson and Bob Dylan, even though they're both shorter than everyone except Paul Simon, who I also look up to.

I see Willie as a storybook gingerbread man: born into poverty, rich in the coin of the spirit, ephemeral and timeless, fragile and strong, beautiful beyond words and music, healing the broken hearts of other people and sometimes, just maybe, his own as well. Yesterday's wine for Willie includes personal tragedies, Internal Revenue Service audits, and a somewhat geriatric band that has been around since Christ was a cowboy yet to this very day undeniably takes no prisoners. The changing landscape of country music has made major-label support and generous radio airplay almost a thing of the past. For many legends of country music, this trendy tidal wave toward Nashville poster boys and modern, youthful "hat acts," plus the inevitable pull of the old rocking chair, has meant the end of careers that were supposed to last forever.

In the midst of all this, like a diamond amongst the rhinestones, Willie Nelson stays on the road.

## EVERYBODY IS SOMEBODY IN LUCKENBACH

During the 1970s, the little burg of Luckenbach, Texas, became a legendary gathering place for musicians, music fans, dancers, and just plain folks. Luckenbach was originally a German community and remained one for most of the twentieth century. In the 1970s, Hondo Crouch bought the tiny town.

Then, as now, it consisted of a small general store with a post office, a dance hall, and a run-down cotton gin. Hondo had a lot of friends in Texas and he loved to invite them to drop by to play music, dance, tell jokes and stories, and toss washers and horseshoes. Many famous musicians also liked to spend time at Luckenbach. Willie Nelson was a frequent visitor and he and Waylon Jennings later recorded a popular song about the town. During the early 1970s, another Hill Country character named Guich Koock served as creative director for a series of Luckenbach World Fairs. These fairs featured chicken flying contests, armadillo races, country music, and "down-home" cooking.

Hondo Crouch has since gone to Jesus, but

Luckenbach continues to be a favorite gathering place for music and dancing. It also hosts the popular Ladies' State Championship Chili Cook-Off.

It was also the venue, in 1973, where Kinky Friedman and the Texas Jewboys performed their very first public concert.

# THE TEXAS CELEBRITY HIGH SCHOOL FOOTBALL HALL OF FAME

### QUARTERBACK:
Larry Gatlin, singer,
Odessa High School Broncos, 1966

★

Rick Perry, Governor of Texas,
Paint Creek School Pirates, 1968.

★

Richard Linklater, filmmaker,
Huntsville High School Hornets, 1976–1978.

★

Jamie Foxx, actor,
Terrell High School Tigers, 1986.

★

### RUNNING BACK:
Patrick Swayze, actor,
Waltrip High School Rams (Houston), 1971.

★

George Strait, singer,
Pearsall High School Mavericks, 1970.

★

**CENTER:**
Bud Shrake, author,
Paschal High School Panthers, 1949.

★

**GUARD:**
Tommy Lee Jones, actor,
Saint Mark's School of Texas Lions (Dallas), 1965.

★

**TACKLE:**
Joe Don Baker, actor,
Groesbeck High School Goats, 1954.

★

**LINEBACKER:**
Stone Cold Steve Austin, professional wrestler,
Edna High School Cowboys.

★

**DEFENSIVE BACK:**
Powers Booth, actor,
Snyder High School Tigers, 1966.

# CHILI, THE STATE DISH

More than a hundred years ago women known as
"chili queens" sold "bowls of red" on the square in
San Antonio. This is the earliest account of chili, the

official state dish of Texas. The recipe began as a way to save money by hashing beef or venison for stew, and there were no vegetables in it—no tomatoes or onions, and never any beans. Today almost every Texan thinks his or her chili recipe is the best, and these declarations are often the source of heated debate.

This notion has led to several annual chili-cooking competitions where Texans can compete to determine who really *is* the best. The first chili cook-off took place in 1967 in the West Texas ghost town of Terlingua. Despite the remote location, 209 chapters of the Chili Appreciation Society sent representatives by car, plane, and school bus. When judges at the cook-off tasted the entries, their faces turned red and they broke out in a heavy sweat. Some judges even fell to the floor, so good were the entries (good equaling hotter 'n hell). No winner was declared at that competition. Since then, musical groups and hordes of partygoers meet in Terlingua each November for the World Championship Chili Cook-Off, where winners are declared and judges emerge, for the most part, unscalded.

What I want to know is how are we gonna
get down to that top soil?

## TEXAS WEATHER

It's so dry in Texas that the cows are giving
evaporated milk.

A Texan once prayed "I wish it would rain—
not so much for me, because I've seen it,
but for my ten year old."

&#9733;

A visitor to Texas once asked, "Does it
ever rain out here?" A rancher answered
"Yes, it does. Do you remember that part in
the Bible where it rained for forty days and
forty nights?" The visitor said "Noah's flood, yes."
"Well," the rancher replied, "we got about
two and half inches out of that."

&#9733;

There was a story about an outsider, probably
from back east, who got miffed because the locals
didn't get too excited one way or the other about
the weather. He noticed that nobody bitched much,
whether it was cold or hot or windy or wet. He said
to one of the locals, "I never hear anyone around
here bitch about the weather. Doesn't it bother you
sometimes?" To which the local responded, "Hell,
don't do no good to bitch. If you don't like the
weather in Texas, just wait a bit. It'll change."

&#9733;

"Jake, now that you've got 'em broke, when does
he go to eatin' outta your hands?"

## SHOSHONE THE MAGIC PONY

**A** happy childhood, I've always believed, is the worst possible preparation for life. Life is so different from childhood, it seems. The magic tricks have all been explained to us. The sparkle, we now realize, is all secondhand smoke and rearview mirrors. Maybe things were always this way, but I don't really think so. I think there was a time.

In 1953, when I was about seven years old, my parents took me to see Shoshone the Magic Pony. That was also the year that Tom and Min Friedman bought Echo Hill Ranch and turned it into a children's camp, providing thousands of boys and girls with many happy, carefree summers of fun. But although 1953 might've been a good year for the Friedmans and a good year for wine, it'd been a bad year for almost everybody and everything else. Hank Williams, along with Julius and Ethel Rosenberg, had checked out of the mortal motel that year, quite possibly unaware that the other party had been there to begin with. Hank fried his brains and heart and

> "A happy childhood . . . is the worst possible preparation for life."

other internal organs for our sins, using eleven different kinds of herbs and spices. Julius and Ethel, charged, many thought falsely, with spying for the Soviet Union, were fried by our government and died declaring their innocence and their love for each other. Hank's songs declared his innocence and his love, inexplicably, for people. It is doubtful whether Hank and the Rosenbergs had anything in common at all, except that a small boy in Texas had cried when each of them died.

The boy had also cried the year before when Adlai Stevenson had lost the potato-sack hop at the company picnic to good ol' Ike, the Garth Brooks of all presidents, who turned out to be the most significant leader we'd had since Millard Fillmore and remained as popular as the bottle of ketchup on the kitchen table of America, even if Lenny Bruce and Judy Garland, who were both destined to die on the toilet, like Elvis, remained in their rooms for the entire two terms of his presidency.

The kid had seemed to cry a bit back then, but fortunately, human tragedies of this sort never cut into his happy childhood. When he grew up, he continued to cry at times, though the tears were no longer visible in or to the naked eye, for he never let human tragedies of this sort cut into his cocktail hour. But during his childhood, it is very likely that his parents noticed the tears. That may have been the reason they took him to see Shoshone the Magic Pony.

These days, as we peer cautiously out across the gray listless afternoon that is adulthood, we seek and we find fewer and fewer surprises in life. What dreams we have are veiled in memory, embroidered in regret. Our minds go back to yesterday street and the summertime of our choosing. Maybe it's 1953. Maybe it's a little rodeo arena near Bandera, Texas, where the loudspeaker had just announced Shoshone the Magic Pony. My father and mother, Tom and Min, were sitting on the splintery bleachers next to me and my little brother Roger. And suddenly, all our eyes were on the center of the arena.

Shoshone came out prancing, led by an old cowboy with a big white beard. He took the reins and bridle off Shoshone and the horse bowed several times to the audience. Shoshone had a beautiful saddle and a large saddle blanket that seemed to glitter with sequins of red, white, and blue. Then the old cowboy stood back and the music began. It was "The Tennessee Waltz." And Shoshone the Magic Pony started to dance.

It was apparent from the outset, even to us children in the crowd,

> **"Our minds go back to yesterday street and the summertime of our choosing."**

> "It was apparent from the outset, even to us children in the crowd, that there were two men inside the body of Shoshone."

that there were two men inside the body of Shoshone. You could tell by the clever, intricate soft-shoe routine she was performing, by the fact that she often appeared to be moving hilariously in two directions at once, and by the funny and very unponylike way she now and again humped and arched her back to the music. I was laughing so hard I forgot for the moment about Hank Williams, Adlai Stevenson, the Rosenbergs, and myself. Whoever was inside there was so good, I even forgot that they were inside there.

Then "The Tennessee Waltz" was over.

Shoshone bowed a deep, theatrical bow. Everybody laughed and clapped and cheered. The old cowboy took off his hat. Then he took off his beard. Then he took off the old cowboy mask he was wearing, and we saw to our amazement that the old-timer was in reality a very pretty young girl.

She took off Shoshone's saddle. Then she took off the saddle blanket. And there, to my total astonishment, stood only Shoshone the Magic Pony.

Shoshone, you see, was a real horse.

In the years that followed, as I grew up or simply got older, Shoshone served me well as a reminder of the duplicitous nature of man and life itself. Nothing is what it appears to be, I thought. But there are times when, with awkward grace, the odd comfort of this crazy world comes inexplicably close to my crazy heart. At times like these, I see Shoshone as a shining symbol of the galloping faith that some horses and some people will always remain exactly who they are.

# THE YELLOW ROSE OF TEXAS

The story of the Yellow Rose of Texas is one of the most enduring legends of the Texas Revolution. According to the legend, Sam Houston sent an attractive mulatto slave named Emily Morgan into the Mexican camp before the Battle of San Jacinto to distract Santa Anna while the Texican Army readied its attack. Santa Anna, who was known to be fond of the company of women, supposedly took the young Emily into his tent, and thus preoccupied, let down his guard. In this version of the battle, Emily Morgan played the role of an 1830s Mata Hari, enabling the Texicans to gain victory at the expense of her virtue.

Since that day when Emily Morgan effectively distracted Santa Anna, she has been immortalized in legend and song as "The Yellow Rose of Texas . . . the sweetest little rosebud that Texas ever knew."

# TENEHA, TIMPSON, BOBO, AND BLAIR

"Teneha, Timpson, Bobo, and Blair" was the conductor's call along the small East Texas rail line in Shelby County. This lyrical quartet of consecutive small towns gave their names to a memorable line in a venerable country-western song, "Teneha, Timpson, Bobo, and Blair, Let Me Get Off Just Any Ole Where."

Texans who fought in World War I introduced others to the four towns as an urgent plea when shooting craps. "Teneha, Timpson, Bobo, and Blair . . . Give me a seven, see if I care."

# THE CONGRESS AVENUE BRIDGE BATS

The largest urban bat colony in North America lives underneath the Congress Avenue bridge in Austin, Texas. Repairs made to the bridge almost twenty years ago created crevices that became a nirvana where bat mothers-to-be could take roost and multiply. Suddenly they moved in by the thousands.

Within five years, so many bats had congregated under the bridge that Austin was starting to take notice in a big way. So large were their numbers that local television stations began showing the bats on weather radar each night.

At the time, Austinites shunned the small creatures, but conservationists pointed out that bats consume up to 30,000 insects nightly, including mosquitoes and agricultural pests, lessening the need for chemical pesticides. Well, Austin would never turn a deaf ear to an environmental appeal. Efforts to eradicate the "pests" screeched to a halt, and a tourist attraction was born.

Batmania has become a part of Austin's culture in a way that would have been unthinkable fifteen years ago. There are bat T-shirts and bat tours; there is a hockey team called the Ice Bats; there are even bat happy hours at bars.

The bats arrive at the bridge in mid-March and return to Mexico in early November, riding the tail wash of the first cold fronts. Tourists and locals gather on both banks of Town Lake or on the bridge's crevices, in preparation for the fall migration. Late summer offers the best time to witness bat flights, which may occur more than an hour before dark and last forty-five minutes, with up to seven columns of bats filling the early evening skies.

Well, I'll be. Been using this bridge fer 20
years and she ain't ever broke before.

## THE MOST FAMOUS TEXAS
## HORNED TOAD

The most celebrated horned toad in the history of
Texas was known as "Old Rip."

In 1897, a justice of the peace named Ernest
Wood was dedicating the cornerstone of the new
Eastland County courthouse.

Along with the usual items sealed in corner-
stones in those days—a Bible, a newspaper, photo-

graphs—Judge Wood put in a large horned toad that his son had been playing with during the ceremony.

In 1928 the old courthouse was being demolished to make way for a new one, and all the local VIPs gathered for the formal opening of the cornerstone. Old Rip's supposedly mummified carcass was recovered along with the rest of the memorabilia. In full view of a large crowd, including city officials, the media, and members of the clergy, the horned toad was found to be alive, although dormant. After being held for a few minutes, the creature began to respond. Old Rip (named after Rip Van Winkle, of course) went on a nationwide tour that included a private audience with President Calvin Coolidge. Unfortunately, Old Rip died after the tour, from complications of pneumonia. The elderly frog was laid to rest in a satin-lined casket in the new Eastland County Courthouse, where he remains to this day.

## CHUCK WAGON COOKING

Stella Hughes lists a cowboy's menu served on a ranch in Northeast Texas, in 1868 or thereabouts:

Roast venison with brown gravy

★

Fried catfish (caught from the river that morning)

★

Squirrel stew

★

Black-eyed peas

★

Corn on the cob

★

Cornbread with fresh churned butter

★

Cold buttermilk

★

Wild honey

★

Plum jam

★

Sliced cucumbers with sour cream

★

Watermelon rind pickles

★

The boss said that we oughta be inspired
by the fact we're developin' the vast
resources of the great West.

## DRAWING FROM EXPERIENCE

In the fall of 1991, a buddy of mine, Jerry Clifton, came up with a great notion: Produce a gala concert in Kerrville starring Ace Reid, the world's greatest cowboy cartoonist, and myself, author, musician, politician, and beautician. Clifton proposed calling the event "Two Legends of Texas Humor."

I talked the whole idea over with Ace, and we both felt that the two of us quite possibly were the most humorous Texans alive. John Henry Faulk and Hondo Crouch were dead, of course, and Ann Richards, Molly Ivins, and Liz Carpenter weren't available, and besides, it wasn't clear if our fellow Kerrverts would find a woman all that humorous.

Ace, as well as being the World's Greatest Cowboy Cartoonist, a title he not undeservedly bequeathed upon himself, was a very complex man, with strong strains of humility and hubris intertwining in the fabric that not only constituted his character but made him one as well. Ace felt that "Two

Legends of Texas Humor" was a bit bland and the two of us entertained another possible title for the gala event: "Two Old Farts in the Night," which I dutifully passed along, so to speak, to Jerry Clifton. Clifton, though not an entirely humorless or constipated type, nonetheless felt that "Two Legends" was the stronger title and went ahead with the printing of tickets and posters for the concert.

"Two Legends of Texas Humor," however, was never meant to be. On a chilly, gray morning in November at a truck stop somewhere in New Jersey, only two weeks before the show was to take place, I learned that Ace Reid had gone to Jesus. Only later did I learn from his wife Madge and from friends who'd known him much longer than I had, how many times Ace had dodged the bullet in his life—beating leukemia in 1961, triumphing over abject poverty, and overcoming the almost inexorable forces that worked to keep him an unfulfilled, unknown cowpoke in Electra, Texas.

Ace Reid beat the odds many times in his life, and not the least of these victories was what he managed to accomplish creatively and professionally. Though Ace's father and family were convinced that art

> **"Ace's name is known far and wide. Mention him to any cowboy or ranchman west of the Mississippi and you'll almost always get a smile."**
>
> **—ELMER KELTON**

was not a suitable occu-
pation for a cowboy, and
though he had little for-
mal education or train-
ing, Ace became without a

**"I was just too dumb to know I couldn't do it."**

doubt the most popular and best-loved cowboy cartoonist in the West. As his friend Elmer Kelton said:
"Ace's name is known far and wide. Mention him to
any cowboy or ranchman west of the Mississippi and
you'll almost always get a smile."

Indeed, Ace could have probably conquered the
lands east of the Mississippi if he'd tried. By 1983
his weekly cartoon series *Cowpokes* was appearing
in well over 500 newspapers, making him the
biggest self-syndicator in the world. By this time he
also had eleven books in print and the Ace Reid
Calendar had become a staple in rural and small-
town banks, hardware stores, groceries, and homes
throughout the West. According to John Erickson,
Ace's biographer, "Officials of the Vernon Company
of Newton, Iowa, publishers of the Ace Reid
Calendars, estimated that in twenty-six years 100
million Ace Reid cartoons have appeared on calendars, making him the most popular calendar artist in
the West today."

But Ace Reid was far more than a cartoonist. He
was a dreamer, a drinker, a character, a prankster,
and a storyteller in the western tradition of Will
Rogers, Mark Twain, and John Henry Faulk. Not

only was Ace the World's Greatest Cowboy Cartoonist and the biggest self-syndicator in the world (he became to the rural West what the cartoonist Bill Mauldin had been to World War II) but he was also much sought after for speaking engagements. And Ace's voice was unique, like the man himself. He spoke with a warm, friendly, booming Panhandle twang that often had a timbre not dissimilar to a barbed-wire fence singing in a dust storm. And this was fitting, for Ace remembered well the dust storms, droughts, and depressions of his youth, and he drew upon these as surely as he drew upon the paper in front of him to triumph over a hard-luck hand.

Ace's family had no electricity or indoor plumbing—only mosquitoes, rattlesnakes, hailstorms, and tornados—and as a youngster Ace sometimes had to work cattle at a temperature of twelve degrees below zero. Ace also recalled walking out of his house one day and watching a man with a gun hijack the postman and his truck as he came to deliver the mail. He learned later that the man was Clyde Barrow.

> "I am the biggest rancher in the world. I have more sheep, horses, and cattle than anyone, and if you don't believe it, I'll sit down and draw 'em."

At age five Ace was already drawing sketches of horses and other animals. In high school he

"Why do cowboys drink so much? Wul, you
would too if your rear end wuz always sore, er
you wuz too hot er too cold and yore pants wuz
always too tight!"

turned a chicken coop into an art studio. In 1943 he
dropped out of high school to join the Navy and see the
world. His cartoons appeared in the ship's paper, but
after the war, instead of heading for the Big Apple, as
some New York correspondents on his ship had suggested, he went back home to Electra. For three years
he tried earning a living in cattle and oil, drawing cowboy cartoons in his spare time. Ace and his wife,
Madge, met in Electra in 1946, and three years later

they eloped to Dallas, shortly after Ace had given up on oil and cattle and had begun selling cartoons to various newspapers. It took three more years of moving around selling art out of their car before they settled in Kerrville, where Ace was the first artist in a town now famous as an art colony.

Ace Reid never had a literary agent. He never had a publishing house. Yet he and Madge brought out thirteen volumes of his cartoons and sold them in countless numbers. Ace never had a public relations firm, but Madge was able to book all the speaking engagements he could possibly want, at $1,500 a night. How did the two of them accomplish all that? Ace's answer: "I was just too dumb to know I couldn't do it." Few people today believe that.

The following is Ace's own account of the time he had a saddle made to give to LBJ about six months after Lyndon had become president:

"Newspaper got wind of what was going on, and I flew into Fort Worth. There was black limosines, there was television cameras, there was newspaper photographers, there was reporters—I was a star! And they carried me to the Fort Worth Press Club, where they had all that stuff set up—cameras, reporters, me getting my picture made. We had everything but the saddle, and it wasn't done.

"They had champagne—I think that's what burned me out on champagne—till one o'clock, and the saddle showed up about one, and by that time I could've cared less if the saddle ever got there.

"Well, at nine o'clock that morning we got aboard that plane and they put the saddle in the

> **"I can't talk New York or Los Angeles, but I can talk the ways of an animal."**

aisle so everybody could see it and they broke out the champagne. We flew into Dulles and there was a car for me, wanted me in Richmond at the *Richmond Leader*. They'd heard that saddle was comin' in and they held up the presses.

"We took off to Richmond and they had the champagne. Damn near made a wino out of me on that trip. We got our pictures in the Richmond paper, got back to D.C. I had congressmen opening the door for me. I had senators carrying the saddle for me. I had senators pulling the corks on those champagne bottles.

"The next morning here was the senators and congressmen knocking on my door, opening that champagne. The limousine was waiting to take us to the White House, with senators opening the doors and carrying the saddle.

"We get to the White House, go through those big old iron gates, and I've got the saddle. But the president of Turkey had beat me there and I had to stand out on that sidewalk slapping those damn pigeons off that saddle. I get inside finally and here comes old Lyndon out, and he says: 'Ace, has it rained down home?' That was the first thing he said.

"We went into the oval room and they took pictures of me and Madge and the president with the saddle, and we left, went out through those iron gates. There wasn't a senator. I walked back to the Willard Hotel. I opened the doors myself. I pulled the snap tops out of them beer cans; there wasn't any more champagne.

"I was a has-been in Washington, D.C., by turning loose of a saddlehorn."

For a cowpoke who never finished high school, Ace Reid left a legacy of work that reflects a highly refined philosophic eye for the human (and animal) condition; he drew with intelligence and imagination and artistry and dignity the simple frustrations of the ordinary man.

His love and understanding of animals also comes across clearly in Ace's work. As the artist himself remarked: "I am the biggest rancher in the world. I have more sheep, horses, and cattle than anyone, and if you don't believe it, I'll sit down and draw 'em . . . I can't talk New York or Los Angeles, but I can talk the ways of an animal."

Ace was a very colorful American, and the people he gathered around him were by all standards an extremely mischievous, fun-loving bunch. One of his closest friends and running mates was the much-celebrated mayor of Luckenbach, Hondo Crouch. Ace and Hondo did the dinner, rodeo, and party circuits together as well as several notorious stints in Las Vegas including one where Hondo was picked up on the strip by the police at two o'clock in the morning, mistaken for a hippie. "Naw," said Hondo. "I got an airplane." Madge Reid had indeed hired a private plane for Hondo, but he had to take the cops to the airport before they'd believe him. What follows is Ace's account of his adventures with Hondo when the Smithsonian Institution invited the newly formed Institute of Texas Cultures to send representatives to Washington in the early 1960s:

> "Ace also once lent a hand at a sold-out lobster party at the Inn of the Hills. When he found out the owner was worried because the lobsters he'd ordered flown in from Maine hadn't arrived yet, Ace filled the bottoms of the lobster tanks with crawfish from the creek at his ranch. One patron was overheard to mutter: 'I wouldn't pay eight dollars for one of those.'"

"We had our Texas culture: Germans from Fredericksburg, we had our Mexicans from San Antone, we had our Czechoslovakians from down around Corpus, we had our Cajuns from East Texas, we had our Indians from out around El Paso.

"Well, old Hondo came by here in his old pickup, picked me up so we could catch the airplane. He had a couple of jugs of tequila and we got to nipping

Well, how wuz I to know? The boss jist
asked: "You want a job where you can
start from the top?"

on that tequila. He had a pillowcase full of German
sausages, all wrapped up. And he had some rattlesnake hides hanging out of the pillowcase with the
rattlers still on the tail.

"We hit that airport. . . . They'd see old Hondo
with the sack of rattlesnakes walking through there,
and he wiggled the neck of that sack and those rattlers would just rattle. They was leaving him alone.

"Then we got on the airplane. They made three mistakes. First, inviting Hondo; second, letting him on the airplane; and third, putting him on the front seat. Everybody had their eyes on Hondo.

"We took off and got about twenty-five thousand feet and old Hondo went to crawling down the aisle on his hands and knees. Sure 'nuff, there was an old fat lady there said: 'Hondo, what are you looking for?' He said, 'Oh, three of my little rattlesnakes got out and I can't find 'em anywhere.'

"That old lady squalled, throwed her legs up in the air, the whole front end of that airplane went to the back end and that plane turned up just like that. Went to thirty-five thousand feet and that pilot fighting those controls and he finally got it trimmed.

"And then he came back to trim old Hondo. He was giving him a very severe talking to and the old pilot grabbed him by the collar and was shaking him. And one old cowboy who was a prickly pear burner from down South Texas, he was part of Texas Cultures, he said: 'You turn that boy loose or I'm gonna throw your butt off this airplane.'

"And that old captain turned around and there was some Cajuns sitting there from the Sabine River, they'd never been higher than a pirogue boat and didn't like that airplane in the first place, one of 'em said: 'Oh, please don't throw heem off, hee's the one that's driving thees theeng!'

"And old captain went in the cockpit, locked the door, and said, 'Je-zuz Christ.' Then he called Dulles airfield that we was coming in and there was a crazy person aboard the airplane. He didn't say it was a crazy man or woman, said it was a crazy person.

"We landed there and American Airlines come in on the other runway, almost wingtip to wingtip. They've got those big old buses that come up to the door and take you up to the terminal. Well, they both hit the terminal at about the same time and the police was swarming. A little old lady got off of Continental ahead of old Hondo and she had her knitting in her little bag, and those police jerked that thing away, stomped hell out of it, broke her knittin' needles, and Hondo scooted through that line and was gone."

But even without Hondo's help Ace was a hard act to follow. In 1965 during hunting season Ace was thrown out of the exclusive Angora Club in Kerrville for taking a buck that a friend had shot into the club, propping it up at the bar, and ordering it a martini. Ace also once lent a hand at a sold-out lobster party at the Inn of the Hills. When he found out the owner was worried because the lobsters he'd ordered flown in from Maine hadn't arrived yet, Ace filled the bottoms of the lobster tanks with crawfish from the creek at his ranch. One patron was overheard to mutter: "I wouldn't pay eight dollars for one of those." In

August of 1965 the
Texas Outdoor Writers'
Association held a big
barbecue at Ace's friend
Charlie Schreiner III's
YO Ranch, with the

**"I think Ace Reid is the soul of Texas."**

—TUMBLEWEED SMITH

guests of honor being Governor John Connally and
Ace Reid. Later, in front of photographers and television cameras, Ace put his arm around the governor
and said: "I want you to know that this is the greatest honor of my life, standing here with Governor Lee
O'Daniel."

My personal experience with the mischief-
loving side of Ace Reid came about five years ago,
when the local cancer society declared a "smokeless day" in Kerrville and Ace and I, as the two
most high-profile Kerrverts available, were tapped
to be smoke-persons for the event. We were both to
be monitored for twenty-four hours, twelve of which
were to be spent autographing our various books
and paraphernalia together in the local mall. And
during this entire time neither of us was to take so
much as a puff of tobacco.

For me the experience was a difficult and
tedious one, since I've smoked about twelve cigars a
day for the past twenty years. I wasn't sure I could
do it and probably wouldn't have done it if Ace hadn't
encouraged and cajoled me and told me, "We'll be in

this thing together." I also wasn't sure what unpleasant effects it might have upon the architecture of my personality.

I made it through the night without smoking, but things began to degenerate that morning when we got to the mall. "We can do it," Ace told me. We signed books and calendars and shook hands with people all day and we didn't smoke. I had headaches and shaky hands, and when I finally said good-bye to Ace, I thought I saw some green spermatozoans swimming around on top of his cowboy hat. Ace himself was steady, even cheerful, during the whole course of the nightmare.

When I got back to the ranch, the first three things I did was light a cigar, pour a shot of Jack Daniels, and call Ace. He wasn't home but Madge answered and I told her that we'd both made it through the smokeless day and to give my congratulations to Ace.

"What for?" she said. "He's never smoked in his life."

There are many ways to remember Ace Reid. Because of the prodigious body of his work Ace's calendars will decorate the walls of the West well into the next century and perpetuate his humor, his wisdom, and his name. But there is something deeper in the man and his legacy to us. As his friend Tumbleweed Smith once put it: "I think Ace Reid is the soul of Texas."

"Yep, Jake, it looks hopeless, but I don't
think it's serious!"

To obtain Ace Reid Calendars, books, or
brochures call 830-257-7446 or write to: Ace Reid
Enterprises, P.O. Box 290868, Kerrville, TX,
78029.

## OUTLAWS IN TEXAS

In the fall of 1876, Billy the Kid broke into the El
Paso County jail to rescue a friend named Melguides

Segura. The Kid rode eighty-one miles to the town. He tricked the prison guard into opening the door by posing as a deputy; he grabbed the jailer's arm and with his revolver persuaded the guard to surrender his handgun and the keys to the jail. He and Segura shackled the two guards on duty to a post outside and rode off into the night.

Dr. John H. "Doc" Holliday, the gambler and gunslinger who was a friend of Wyatt Earp, once practiced dentistry in the city of Dallas. Wyatt Earp and Doc Holliday first met in Fort Griffin, Texas. It was in Fort Griffin that Doc Holliday was busted out of jail by his lady friend, the prostitute Big Nose Kate.

Butch Cassidy and the Sundance Kid, along with their gang, the "Hole in the Wall Gang" (or the "Wild Bunch"), holed up at Fannie Porter's brothel in Fort Worth while being pursued by law posses and Pinkerton detectives.

While in Fort Worth, the boys passed a photographer's studio and decided to have a group portrait made. The photographer, not knowing the identity of his subjects, posted a copy of the photo in his window as advertisement for his studio. A Pinkerton detective noticed the photo and recognized the gang. He alerted the posse, and the gang fled. Butch and Sundance went to South America, where they were eventually killed by soldiers.

The notorious gunman John Wesley Hardin was shot in the back by John Selman, Sr., in 1895 in the Acme Saloon in El Paso, Texas.

## ROUGH RIDERS

The famous "Rough Riders" of Teddy Roosevelt were trained at the Bexar County Exposition grounds in San Antonio, Texas. Many of them signed up on the Alamo grounds or in the nearby Menger Hotel. One hundred and twenty-seven Texans made up a major part of the Rough Riders. They were the first volunteer cavalry regiment that enlisted, and they were quartered in the exposition hall.

"Shake, pardner. I'm always glad to meet a couple of genuine cowboys like myself."

# WANTED: THE REAL URBAN COWBOY

*To tell you the truth this telephone booth gets*
    *lonesome in the rain.*
    *But son, I'm twenty-one in Nashville and I'm*
    *forty-three in Maine*
*And when your mama gets home would you*
    *tell her I phoned—*
    *it'd take a lifetime to explain*
*That I'm a country-picker with a bumper-*
    *sticker that says 'God Bless John Wayne.'*

—"THE PEOPLE WHO READ PEOPLE MAGAZINE"

**T**he life of a country singer can at times be very tedious. You have to pretend that your life is a financial pleasure even when your autographs are bouncing.

You fall prey to the Jackson Downe Southern California songwriters' self-pity syndrome. You begin to believe that all dentists and married couples are happier than you are.

Many's the night you feel lonely, empty, homesick

"You have to pretend that your life is a financial pleasure even when your autographs are bouncing."

for heaven. Everybody you know thinks you've really got it made and suddenly you find you're a jet-set Gypsy cryin' on the shoulder of the highway . . .

New York is a Negro talking to himself. Los Angeles is a VCR with nothing to put in it. And there's a long, long trail a-windin' into the land of your wet, slow-moving, American dreams.

Unlike many of my colleagues in country music, I did not have a childhood that was particularly conducive to country music stardom. I never had the spiritual advantages of having been born the son of a poor, struggling Arkansas dirt farmer. As I grew up, no one ever laughed and pointed at me and said, "Hey, look—there goes the coal miner's daughter."

I never even served any time in prison. Nor did I at any time seek to fabricate such a prison background. For I knew that *my* prison would be walking through this world always having to listen to Eagles albums.

I grew up in the Texas Hill Country, rooting passionately for Adlai Stevenson, the Chicago White Sox, and Sugar Ray Robinson and listening faithfully to Hank Williams, Jimmie Rodgers, and Slim Whitman. I felt for Slim Whitman with his mustache and his memories, yodeling love songs for some long-lost lady yesterday. I shivered for Jimmie Rodgers, the Singin'

Brakeman, standing in the rain waiting for fast freights and faithless women who never came, who finally sang the T.B. blues, dying out like a train whistle in the night, the lantern still swinging in his hand.

And Hank Williams—skinny, hungry, spiritually horny, for whom all the world was a stage. Shakespeare of the sequined summer stock. Hank Williams died when he was twenty-nine years old—perfect timing for a country music legend. Hank and Jimmie both made it to hillbilly heaven on roller skates before I could ever sit around and swap songs with them, but I did get to meet Slim Whitman once. He was sitting in a Holiday Inn, eating ice cream and wearing red socks.

Years later a friend of mine, Rick Goldberg, was to send me a personally autographed photo of Slim that read: "Best Wishes to the Friedmans—Good Luck, Slim Whitman." I put Slim right away into my Whitman Family Album side by side with his two highly celebrated brothers, Walt and Charles.

I am always a bit reluctant to open my hope chest too widely. I fear too many Americans may seek to peek into the secret pockets of my youth. Nonetheless, I will allow that over the years I've managed to collect three other treasured autographs that I only pray will not bounce: Ernest

> "I never had the spiritual advantages of having been born the son of a poor, struggling Arkansas dirt farmer."

Tubb's, Abbie Hoffman's, and Lowell George's (the lead singer and spiritual force behind Little Feat).

I got Ernest's when I was only fourteen years old, at the famous Skyline Club in Austin, Texas.

Abbie Hoffman's autograph reads, "To Kinky Friedman—the best Jewish singer since Moses." Well, only time will tell.

Lowell George once autographed a book and gave it to me in Hollywood. The book was titled *How Much Prayer Should a Hamburger Get?* This was shortly before he made it to hillbilly heaven on roller skates.

Lowell had been taking me for a drive through the Hollywood hills in his new Blazer. He apparently had bought that particular vehicle with the royalties from his latest album. He said, in somewhat conspiratorial tones, "You see this Blazer, Kinky? This is what they give you for a gold record." Then we pulled up to a large, sprawling house where Keith Moon's beautiful white Rolls Royce was parked out in front. "That," said Lowell, "is what they give you for a platinum record."

> "I shivered for Jimmie Rodgers, the Singin' Brakeman, standing in the rain waiting for fast freights and faithless women who never came, who finally sang the T.B. blues, dying out like a train whistle in the night, the lantern still swinging in his hand."

"Shore he's a workin' cowboy. I just saw him
work a banker into makin' another payment
on his diamond ring and his Cadillac."

I had attended college at the University of Texas—
in Austin (a severe personal liability; to overcome it
required my taking enormous quantities of rocket
beans and staying up once for five years in a row in
Nashville, Tennessee). I majored in classics and
jungle languages. But what really got me into history,

> *"My* prison would be walking through this world always having to listen to Eagles albums."

country music, and a lot of unpleasant situations was a course called "The Romantic Poets: Were They Philosophers or Fools, and Did They Get Any on Them?" My final thesis compared the symbolism of Elizabeth Barrett Browning's "How Do I Love Thee, Let Me Count the Ways" with Mel Tillis's "I Got the Hoss and You Got the Saddle, Let's Ride, Ride, Ride." Now I could have been a happy orthodontist or a carefree proctologist, but I could hear country music in all my Freudian dreams. One day Nashville beckoned to me.

Soon after I got to Nashville, I realized that a special version of the Bible exists—the Five Books of Music Row. These books, of course, are:

1. Songs: published, unpublished, potential dentist's office appeal.

2. Numbers: listed, unlisted, men's room wall.

3. Profits: false, hidden, not to be followed.

4. The Gospel According to Chet Atkins: Honor thy producer and thy publisher. Remember thy label and keep it country. Deliver us from Eagles, Lord. Don't covet thy neighbor's ass, just please get your ass out of my office. So it is written and so it shall be recorded and so long, sucker.

5. Revelations: Columbus just arriving at the Bank
of America discovers he's overdrawn. Willie,
Waylon, George Jones, and almost every other
great artist discover they are getting hosed by
their record companies and managers a lot more
than by their groupies. Freddy Fender discovers, quite by accident at a crowded party, that
Dolly Parton has "great big ol' titties." Charley
Pride discovers he's a Negro.

A handful of hillbilly heretics believed not and refused
to bow down to these false idols. Soon these bibles
were simply being called "the trades." The Nashville
sound was no longer only the sound of the silent
majority—and the hillbilly
heretics were known as
the "outlaws." Tompall
Glaser of the Glaser brothers opened his studio to
many of us with weird
songs, ideas, and hours.
He and Waylon started
making some real music.
Tompall, who never fit
into Nashville's white-
shoe world, once took my
fairly wiggy cowboy hat
while we played pinball.
He wore it two years and

> " 'You see this Blazer,
> Kinky? This is what they
> give you for a gold record.'
> Then we pulled up to a
> large, sprawling house
> where Keith
> Moon's beautiful white
> Rolls Royce was
> parked out in front.
> 'That,' said Lowell, 'is
> what they give you for a
> platinum record.' "

> "Sorry, chief," he said to the young songwriter, "nobody wants to hear a song about an old drunk nigger and his dog."

then gave it to Waylon. Soon everyone was wearing hats and swapping them like song lyrics. In restaurants where you never before could have entered wearing a hat, you now felt naked without one. Tompall claims that that pinball moment when he took my hat and put it on his head without even tilting was the moment the outlaw movement spiritually began. "Bill Monroe and Ernest Tubb, of course," he noted respectfully, "had always worn them."

Some of us were crucified on crosses of vinyl. We were stoned for our ideas; stoned for our hairy, scary, soon to be legendary lifestyles; or just plain stoned. Billy Joe Shaver wrote "Honky Tonk Heroes," and we were. Lee Clayton wrote "Ladies Love Outlaws," and they did. Willie had been wandering like a modern-day Moses in the Texas desert. Waylon had been a rebel without a clause in his recording contract to say and sing what he believed. And in Austin, Jerry Jeff Walker had just thrown his new color TV set into his swimming pool.

Of course in the Church of the Latter-day Businessman, where souls and careers were saved simultaneously, good ol' boys still got down on their clean-cut, commercially oriented, Christian kneecaps and actually prayed for their song to climb the charts on Jacob's ladder and maybe become one of the top ten commandments.

My first album, *Sold American,* which was produced by Tompall's brother Chuck and released in 1973, was hailed by some as a snowplow of the outlaw movement. It contained these prophetic lyrics from "Flying Down the Freeway":

> *We'll pass the pipe of peace in our adobe*
> *Wrapped up in the flag to keep us warm*
> *We'll dip some snuff and mainline guacomole*
> *Rolling Ronnie Reagan in suppository form.*

On the airwaves, the first voices of Radio Free Redneck—Captain Midnite in Nashville, Sammy Allred and Joe Gracey in Austin—were putting their balls on the turntables by playing "progressive country." By this time, the good ol' boy was practically a dodo bird. A great many writers, critics, artists, and record execs were rooting for Jesse James and his gang. Indeed, the outlaws did get the gold before they began fighting among themselves.

But things had changed in Music City forever. Jerry Jeff Walker had once knocked on every publisher's door in Nashville trying to publish a song he had written called "Mr. Bojangles." Today

> **"If you ain't crazy, there's something wrong with you."**

it's an all-time standard. Back on Music Row then, it was still the dark ages. When Walker played the song for the president of one of the largest, most powerful publishing houses on Music Row, the Music Row magnate, who shall remain nameless and faceless, probably forever—shook his head sagely, looked across his vast mahogany desk, and succinctly summed up everything that was so wrong, so self-righteous, so out of touch, and so out of tune about the Nashville Sound. "Sorry, chief," he said to the young songwriter, "but nobody wants to hear a song about an old drunk nigger and his dog."

On New Year's Eve several years ago I found myself in Houston, Texas, with Little Feat playing one side of town at the same time as Willie and Waylon were performing on the other side of town. I, like many Houstonians, felt pulled in both directions at once. I didn't know whether to kill myself or go bowling. I wound up making a P.A. (public appearance) at the Willie and Waylon concert and getting to the Little Feat show just in time to hear Lowell

> "In Texas . . . we all share the common religious belief that if we live a good life, when we die we go to Willie Nelson's house."

calling me up on the
stage to add a little local
color. He sang: "Give
me weed, whites, and
wine / show me a sign /
and I'll be willin'. . ." I
threw in a little patented
castrati harmony and then

> "You can pick your friends
> and you can pick your
> nose, but you can't wipe
> your friends off on your
> saddle."

it was twelve o'clock and we gaily rang down the curtain on what had to have been, by all accounts, one of
the most repellent years in recent memory.

In the early hours of that morning, I took Lowell
over to the hotel where Willie and Waylon were staying. We got on the elevator at about 5:30 A.M. and
were surprised to find it going down instead of up.
When it stopped, a little spinning ghost with a red
bandana wrapped around its head got aboard. It was
Willie. I introduced them; they shook hands and
smiled at each other. Two of the most beautiful
smiles in America. I said: "Two great hands meet."

Actually Willie had lent me a hand on several
occasions. Once a Dallas club owner and his redneck
robots had escorted me from the stage to the alley.
Later, just as I was preparing to hang from the shower
rod in my hotel room, the phone rang. It was Willie.
Two days later I was sharing the stage with Willie,
Waylon and Leon Russell, looking out at 20,000
drunk and delirious Texans. Willie invited me out to

his house later that night. (In Texas, you understand, we all share the common religious belief that if we live a good life, when we die we go to Willie Nelson's house.)

Willie's house was on a dusty, secret little road. There were no signs on the highway. No stars in the sky. No shoes, no shirt, no service. I was on a pre-C.B. road to Damascus. Willie's vague, dreamlike directions were running through my mind like a rhyming roadmap: "A little south of Austin, a little east of Eden, left at the spiritual crossroads, and then through the mother-of-pearl gates."

I found Willie sitting in his bedroom with nothing but a guitar and a smile. He nodded and laughed. It made me feel very peaceful. He began to glow like some Jesus of the Jukebox. "Am I crazy, Willie?" I looked him straight in the eye. "That's all I want to know." I'll never never forget him standing there, his eyes twinkling with pure bullshit Zen wisdom. "Kinky," he chuckled, "take it from me: If you ain't crazy, there's something wrong with you."

It serves no useful purpose to say who was more fucked up at that late hour in our lives. We were just three Americans alone together in an elevator. Like three wise men following a star. Like three bachelors with our very souls embroidered into the tortured tapestry of some cosmic dating game, we rode up into the night. Why was this night different from all other nights?

I couldn't remember and I couldn't forget. I

couldn't very well ask the other passengers. (Willie'd dropped out of school very early. By day he'd sold Bibles door-to-door to Baptists in Waco. By night he'd sold hubcaps to backslidin' whiskey-palians. Lowell had dropped out before his Mom could finish packing his first lunch pail.)

By this time I was feeling like three sheets in the wind from the Holiday Inn: cried in, lied in, fucked in, and tucked in with mental-hospital corners.

I was never one to get too cosmic, but it did cross my desk then that in some warped dimension of time, Hank Williams was probably dreaming his last back-seat dreams in the backseat of that shimmering, earth-bound Cadillac, on his way to that show in Canton, Ohio, he would never get to play. Some people will do anything to get out of a gig in Canton, Ohio.

Waylon Jennings is probably one of my all-time favorite Americans. He's humorous and magical and he sings "McArthur's Park" better than Richard Harris or Donna Summer or just about anybody else. It would take somebody like Tom Waits or Nina Simone to sing it any better, and then it'd still be pretty close by the time it got to Phoenix.

Once I was walking down a dusty alley and a big Cadillac drove up in a cloud of dust with Waylon at the wheel. He gave me some words to live by—

Man, this is better'n being rich—jist owe
everybody so much they gotta be nice to you.

words I have, to this day, never forgotten. He said:
"Get in, Kink. Walkin's bad for your image."

I don't think the urban cowboy is just passing
through. He's a modern mosaic—Hollywood cowboy, drugstore cowboy, midnight cowboy, outlaw.
Who is this metaphysical masked man? This legendary what's-his-name riding through the desert on
a horse with no legs, swinging his neon lariat?

Here's to you, Lash LaRue, you never moved to Malibu. And Spade Cooley and Lefty Frizzell and Tom Mix and George Jones—they live in our hearts —let the Oak Ridge Boys live on the charts.

The urban cowboy may like Kenny Rogers and Linda Ronstadt more than Hank Williams. But times and trends and program directors change. Four years ago Kenny Rogers was broke; he put on his cowboy hat and now he's fartin' through silk. John Wayne won his first Oscar when he played a guy with an eye patch in *True Grit*. He said, "Hell, if I'd known that, I'd have put on that damn eye patch fifty-four movies ago."

I performed on the Grand Ol' Opry stage long after Hank Williams's teardrops had dried. He was a cowboy, too, and he was never afraid to cry. It was only a few years ago that the Grand Ol' Opry received a fan letter from someone in Japan. The writer said he had collected many American country albums. Country-western was his favorite music, and anytime a country star came to Japan he had always tried to see the show.

"P. S." he had written, "When will Mr. Hank Williams come to play here?"

Believe it or not, I believe in the urban cowboy. (Not the flick, not the trend, not even the high rodeo drag.) But in his wild innocence, his restless spirit, and his dusty dreams. Is he for real?

The urban cowboy may just be as real as a ghost

rider in the American Dream. Of course, I believe in ghosts and American Dreams. A sure sign of success: The dressing room after the show was crowded with fans, celebs, shirttail cousins, groupies, and purveyors of Peruvian marching powder. In the corner, an LA coke dealer, a Georgia faith healer, a Boy Scout, and a junked-out Joan of Arc were freebasing and rolling a couple of Marlboro Lights. Now I've got a million friends, but I'll always remember what George M. Jones once told me: "You can pick your friends and you can pick your nose, but you can't wipe your friends off on your saddle."

> Now if you're too New York for Texas, too
>     Texas for LA
> If you been chasin' trends like rainbow ends
>     but you're always just a song away,
> And if the White House wouldn't have you,
>     play in every little honky-tonk and bar
> You see, the good Lord made the heavens—but
>     He never made a star . . .
> No, it's the People Who Read People Magazine
> It's the soap-opera lovers, it's the hometown
>     bowling team,
> It's everybody everywhere who's ever lost a
>     dream,
> It's the People Who Read People—
>     Who Read People Magazine.

# STILL MORE HOMETOWN HEROES

1. Roger Miller           Fort Worth
2. Lyle Lovett            Klein
3. Bonnie Parker          Rowena
4. Clyde Barrow           Telico
5. George Forman          Marshall
6. Rex Reed               Fort Worth
7. Syd Charisse           Amarillo
8. Debbie Reynolds        El Paso
9. Alvin Ailey            Rogers
10. Aaron Spelling        Dallas
11. Johnny Mathis         Gilmer
12. Gene Autry            Tioga
13. Fess Parker           Fort Worth
14. Ernie Banks           Dallas
15. Sam Donaldson         El Paso

# DAN BLOCKER

Dan Blocker, who played the character Hoss Cartwright in the popular television show *Bonanza,* was born in O'Donnell, Texas. He was the biggest baby ever born in Bowie County, tipping the scales at an impressive fourteen pounds. By the age of nine, he was six feet tall.

# THE COWBOY COOK'S PRAYER

Lord God, You know us old cowhands is forgetful. Sometimes I can't even recollect what happened yestiddy. We is forgetful. We just know daylight and dark, summer, fall, winter, and spring. But I sure hope we don't ever forget to thank You before we is about to eat a mess of good chili.

We don't know why, in Your wisdom. You been so doggone good to us. The heathen Chinee don't have no chili, ever. The Frenchmens is left out. The Rooshians don't know no more about chili than a hog does about a sidesaddle. Even the Meskins don't get a good whiff of it unless they stay around here.

Chili eaters is some of Your chosen people. We

don't know why You so doggone good to us. But
Lord, God, don't ever think we ain't grateful for this
chili we about to eat.

Amen.

—ATTRIBUTED TO BONES HOOKS, A BLACK COWBOY
COOK AT A RANCH REUNION, AND QUOTED BY FRANK
TOLBERT IN *A BOWL OF RED*, 1972.

"Before we git down to this hoss's fine qualities, jist what qualities you wantin'?"

# GOD'S OWN COWBOYS

Last weekend, Barry Goldwater, Chuck Conners ("The Rifleman"), and James Drury ("The Virginian") were inducted into the National Cowboy Hall of Fame in Oklahoma City. Without taking away from this trio's status as fine Americans, one must wonder if the inductors might not have reached a bit spiritually in calling them cowboys.

Far be it for me to suggest that they were not cowboys, for cowboys come in all colors and denominations. My only contention is that the final arbiters of what is a cowboy should be God and small children, and I'm not certain they would have chosen this particular trinity. But let us explore this wandering trail together.

Though Spanish-speaking peoples, it should be noted, are quite often mean to bulls, they did give us the first rodeos in Mexico, in the 1700s. In fact, much of what was to become the cowboy derived from the Spanish vaquero. The first rodeos as we know them in the United States came about a century later and often featured black cowboys. The Cowboy Hall of Fame tells me that its "minority category" (in which all cowboys actually belong) consists of "two Mexicans, two black cowboys, one Native American, and no cowboys recognized as Jewish."

Tom Mix, who is a member, was said to be half-Jewish, and Wyatt Earp was married to a Jewish dance hall girl—but close counts only in horseshoes. Being Jewish and having lived in the Texas Hill Country

Son, you'll never be a good cowboy unless you
can tell when one more piece of balin' wire will
break a shed down!

most of my life, the only thing I've seen that Jews and cowboys seem to have in common is that both wear their hats indoors and attach a certain amount of importance to it.

One of the few real cowboys I know is a man named Earl Buckelew, who has lived all his life in the heart of the Hill Country near Medina, Texas. For more than seventy-six years, Earl has lived on the land, ridden the range, and loved and understood

> **"The final arbiters of what is a cowboy should be God and small children."**

> **"Being Jewish and having lived in the Texas Hill Country most of my life, the only thing I've seen that Jews and cowboys seem to have in common is that both wear their hats indoors and attach a certain amount of importance to it."**

horses. And, what is even rarer, he loves and understands himself. These days, Earl lives in a trailer and watches *Wheel of Fortune.* He was not inducted into the Cowboy Hall of Fame, but then Nellie Fox hasn't made it into the Baseball Hall of Fame yet either.

The notion of the cowboy has always been one of America's most precious gifts to the children of the world. Indeed, the early cowboys, whether they drove down the Chisholm Trail or Sunset Boulevard, reached higher into the firmament than they might have known. When Anne Frank's secret annex was revisited after World War II, pictures of American cowboy stars were still fluttering from the walls where she had left them.

True cowboys must be able to ride beyond time and geography. They must leave us a dream to grow by, a haunting echo of a song, a fine dust that is visible for generations against even a black-and-white sunset. Today many children of the dust dream of becoming cowboys. And it's OK to think you're a cowboy, unless, of course, you happen to run into someone who thinks he's an Indian.

The trouble with this big ole ranch is there
ain't anyplace to ever take a short cut!